DIVER'S GUIDE
TO THE
KITCHEN

To Stephanie,
Dive in & get cookin'!

Joan Forsberg

DEDICATION

To my daughters, Jennifer and Lara,
who always ate what I cooked
and smiled throughout

DIVER'S GUIDE TO THE KITCHEN

Compiled and Edited by

Joan Forsberg

West Chicago

DIVER'S GUIDE TO THE KITCHEN
BY JOAN FORSBERG

COPYRIGHT © 2003 SEAWOLF COMMUNICATIONS, INC.

ALL RIGHTS RESERVED

ISBN 0-9679976-3-1

LIBRARY OF CONGRESS CONTROL NUMBER: 2003091539

SEAWOLF COMMUNICATIONS, INC.
PO BOX 66
WEST CHICAGO, IL 60186
USA

Tel: (630) 293-8996   Fax: (630) 293-8837
www.seawolfcommunications.com

NOTE: All photographs in this book are by **Cris Kohl,** unless otherwise noted in a caption below the photo, and are © Seawolf Communications, Inc.
Submitted photos are marked as such. These images are © by their photographers.

Printed on recycled paper and bound in the United States of America

FIRST EDITION: JUNE, 2003

5 4 3 2 1

FRONT COVER: *Center Photo*---Underwater explorers prepare for a fine meal: **Ralph White** *(left)* lists the underwater cinematography for the most successful film in the world, *Titanic*, among his many subaquatic credits. **Joyce Hayward** *(center)*, a member of the Women Divers' Hall of Fame, remains a stabilizing force as the "Queen Bee of the Great Lakes." **Robert Marx** *(right)* is the world's leading expert on underwater treasure research and salvage, and is the author of more than 40 books. For their respective recipes, see pages 100, 30 and 80. *Background Photo*---Blue waters off Waikiki, Hawaii. (PHOTOS BY CRIS KOHL)

BACK COVER: Contributors to this cookbook include well-known figures in the scuba world *(clockwide from upper left):* **Zale Parry** (PHOTO BY CRIS KOHL), **John Chatterton** (PHOTO SUBMITTED BY JOHN CHATTERTON), **Teddy Tucker** (PHOTO BY ELLSWORTH BOYD), **Jack & Sue Drafahl** (PHOTO SUBMITTED BY JACK & SUE DRAFAHL), **Danielle Alary & Michel Gilbert** (PHOTOS SUBMITTED BY DANIELLE ALARY & MICHEL GILBERT), and **Dr. Robert Ballard** (PHOTO BY CRIS KOHL). *Lower left:* **Joan Forsberg,** editor. (PHOTO BY CRIS KOHL)

INTRODUCTION

I love to cook!

I am a sprawling, over-the-top, around-the-bend, shiver-the-timbers, cook-at-the-top-of-my-lungs cook. When I get creative in the kitchen, I use every dish and pan in the house -- pots steaming, grease dripping, splatters flying. Leftovers at my house have a different meaning -- it's what's left over on the floors, on the walls and on the ceiling after the cooking wars. One day, I tried to find my way through the debris field after a dinner party and thought, "I need a diver's guide to the kitchen." After all, there are Diver's Guides to almost every place on earth, and I'll need cave lights, a hardhat, and wreck penetration certification to ever get this kitchen usable again.

The idea stayed in my head and I wondered if we really are what we eat and are we also what we cook? Are divers as adventurous in the kitchen as they are in the water? I set about to find out, and started collecting recipes from famous people in the world of scuba diving. I began to realize that it wasn't so much the food and its method of preparation, it was most often the story behind it that gave the dish its special meaning. With apologies to the great cookbook writers of the world, this book has a different purpose: to tell a bit about the personal side of these scuba celebrities through the experiences connected to a particular favorite dish of theirs.

The food in this book is as varied as the people themselves, but aside from the fact that they are all divers, they have something else in common. They are all educators. Some are acclaimed photographers, filmmakers and writers, sharing what they've seen and learned in the lakes, rivers and oceans of the world. Through their images and their words, they have taken us to places too deep, too far, or too long ago that we can only dream about. Others have achieved great technical knowledge or accomplished great pioneering feats or have taught us how to be better divers. Some are involved in the organization of the many scuba shows, where divers congregate to learn more about the underwater world. The people in this book are the ones you see doing the presentations, teaching the workshops, and working behind the scenes to make it all happen. These scuba celebrities don't keep their hard-won knowledge to themselves, they share it with all of us, and that's what makes them stars.

Joan Forsberg
High Lake, Illinois
March, 2003

ACKNOWLEDGEMENTS

I thank the following contributors for their recipes and for graciously sharing their personal stories. This is their book:

Rick Allen & Cindy Burnham, Art Bachrach, Robert Ballard, Jonathan Bird, Nancy & Larry Boucha, Jim Bowden, Dick Boyd, Ellsworth Boyd, Georgienne Bradley & Jay Ireland, Ernie Brooks, Jesse Cancelmo, John Chatterton, Gary Chesnut, Bernie Chowdhury, Dan Crowell, Ned & Anna DeLoach, Jack & Sue Drafahl, Glenn Egstrom, Tom Farnquist, Jeri & Chuck Feltner, Dennis Gagnon, Gary Gentile, Michel Gilbert & Danielle Alary, Bret Gilliam, Jeff Gray, Bill Hamilton, Patrick Hammer, Joyce Hayward, Karl Huggins, Paul Humann, Hank Keatts, Cris Kohl, Emory Kristoff, Ann Kristovich, Ryan LeBlanc, Dan Lenihan, Steve Lewis, Bob Marx, Pete Nawrocky, Valerie Olson Van Heest, Dan & Betty Orr, Zale Parry, Adam Ravetch, Vreni Roduner, Bob Sanders, Brian Skerry, Wes Skiles, Kimm Stabelfeldt, Jim & Pat Stayer, Bill Steinborn, Dave Trotter, Teddy Tucker, Mike & Georgann Wachter, Dan Wagner, Stan Waterman, Hal Watts, Ralph White and Mike Williams.

For submitted photos from Bob Allen, Rick Allen & Cindy Burnham, Jonathan Bird, Larry & Nancy Boucha, Ellsworth Boyd, Georgienne Bradley & Jay Ireland, Ernest Brooks, Jesse Cancelmo, John Chatterton, Gary Chesnut, Chet Childs, Jack & Sue Drafahl, Dennis Gagnon, Michel Gilbert & Danielle Alary, Bret Gilliam, Hank & Carole Keatts, Joe Oliver, Dan & Betty Orr, Zale Parry, Adam Ravetch, Vreni Roduner, Bob Sanders, Brian Skerry, Kimm Stabelfeldt, Bill Steinborn, Mike & Georgann Wachter, Hal Watts, Stan Waterman, Ralph White, Mike Williams and Chris Winters, I am very grateful.

An intensely heartfelt thank you to:

Kate Kauffman and Kate Thompson of NOAA's Thunder Bay Underwater Sanctuary and Preserve at Alpena, Michigan, Dianna Chowdhury, Carole Keatts, Jenifer Marx and Edna Tucker for seeing to it that I received recipes or more information in time for publication;

The small army of "official tasters" who helped me test recipes in this book: Donna Ayers, my daughter, Lara Hernandez Corkrey (who also helped proofread), Georgia Hamilton, Pat Moore, Penny Salvesen and Marsha Steinbrecher;

Jim and Pat Stayer for their patient assistance with the covers of this book;

The divers on the front cover of this book, Ralph White, Joyce Hayward, and Bob Marx who were such good sports.

Most of all, I thank my husband, Cris Kohl, for advice, enthusiasm, hard work, and a kick in the rear when I needed it. There would have been no book without him.

CONTENTS

INTRODUCTION 5
ACKNOWLEDGEMENTS 6
CONTENTS 7

First Course: Dive Boat Cuisine 9
STEVE LEWIS' Voodoo Onion Hummus 10
PAUL HUMANN's Mango Manor Salsa 12
RYAN LeBLANC's Isle Royale Dip 14
JERI & CHUCK FELTNER's Tuna Surprise 16
GARY GENTILE's Open Water Banana Split 18
BILL STEINBORN's Flavor Craver Shrimp Dip 20

Second Course: Soups, Salads, Sandwiches 21
BERNIE CHOWDHURY's Moon Chowder 22
ART BACHRACH's Hot Lips Soup with Shrimp and Pork 24
ADAM RAVETCH's Chunky Natsiq Soup 26
PATRICK HAMMER's Key West Clam Chowder 28
JOYCE HAYWARD's New England Clam Chowder 30
TOM FARNQUIST's Whitefish Point Whitefish Chowder 32
NED & ANNA DeLOACH's Bimini Slaw 34
CRIS KOHL's Slaw 36
ZALE PARRY's Diver's Delight Cucumbers 38
BILL HAMILTON's World Class Tomato Sandwich 40
BRIAN SKERRY's Survival Grilled Cheese Sandwich 42
GARY CHESNUT's Savory Salmon Sandwich 44

Third Course: Catch of the Day 45
ROBERT BALLARD's IFE New England Clam Bake 46
BRET GILLIAM's Outdoor Steamed Lobster, Maine Style 48
ELLSWORTH BOYD's Bahama Island Lobster Boats 50
PETE NAWROCKY's Breakdown Smorgasbord 52
JACK DRAFAHL's Bachelor Delight 54
SUE DRAFAHL's Salmon & Loosen-Your-Weightbelt Sauce .. 55
ERNEST BROOKS' Scallops a la "Just Love" 56
HENRY KEATTS' Long Island Scalloped Scallops 58
DAN CROWELL's Fried Smelt, Greek Style 60

TEDDY TUCKER's Hashed Shark 62
RICK ALLEN AND CINDY BURNHAM's Shrimp and Grits 64
DAN & BETTY ORR's DCS (Diver's Chili with Shrimp) 66
WES SKILES' "Hey Now!" Special Sauce 68
GLEN EGSTROM's Razzle-Dazzle Sizzling Fish 70
DAN WAGNER's "FishyDan's" Delight 72
DENNIS GAGNON's Barbecued Narc-ed Fish 74
DAN LENIHAN's Old Baywatch Delight (camping version) ... 76
MIKE & GEORGANN WACHTER's Perfect Perch/Abalone 78
BOB MARX's "For Treasure and Pleasure" Sea Bass 80
DICK BOYD's Campfire Whitefish 82

FOURTH COURSE: LANDLUBBER ENTRÉES 83
DAVE TROTTER's Road Kill Venison Stew 84
VRENI RODUNER's Chicken in Cream Sauce 86
JEFF GRAY's Beer Butt Chicken 88
VALERIE OLSON VAN HEEST's Sterts 90
JESSE CANCELMO's Flower Gardens Eggplant Parmigiana 92
KARL HUGGINS' Rapid Ascent Spaghetti Sauce 94
JONATHAN BIRD's Stuffed Shells and Garlic Bread 96
JIM & PAT STAYER's Too-Many-Divers-in-the-House Chili ... 98
RALPH WHITE's Mixed Gas Chili & Beans (Titanic version) 100
MIKE WILLIAMS' Zesty Mariner's Meatloaf 102
STAN WATERMAN's Peerless Meatloaf 104
EMORY KRISTOFF's "Red Meat Diver's" Steak 106
HAL WATTS' Steak To Dive For 108
JIM BOWDEN's Steak and Seduction 110
BOB SANDERS' South Pole-ish Pork 112
ANN KRISTOVICH's Smokin' Ribs 114

Fifth Course: Desserts 115
JOHN CHATTERTON's Cut-The-Cheese Cheesecake 116
MICHEL GILBERT & DANIELLE ALARY's Eggs in Maple Syrup. 118
GEORGIENNE BRADLEY's Jungle Punch Jello 120
JAY IRELAND's Mom's Tea Ring 121
NANCY AND LARRY BOUCHA's Purple Smile Blueberry Pie .. 122
KIMM STABELFELDT's Chocolate Chip Cookies 124

After-Dinner Mints 125

Index 126

FIRST COURSE: DIVE BOAT CUISINE

Scuba divers take along all kinds of food when they step on board a dive boat for the day, or even for a few hours. In tropical locales, dive boats often offer their wet customers something between dives to remove the saltwater taste from their mouths: orange or pineapple slices, for example. Elsewhere, alternatives are found.

In the Great Lakes, for example, Cris Kohl [See Cris' recipe on page 36] often takes along lots of garlic pickles, sliced into spears and placed in a ziplock bag, for distribution among the underwater adventurers on board, as a way of spicing up that "freshwater flavor" in their mouths. Of course, it works, and it's surprisingly good!

Hawaii dive boat snacks.

Dave Trotter [see Dave's recipe on page 84] reports: "Dr. Werner Wahl takes great pleasure in eating hogshead cheese, roquefort cheese, pickeled pigs' feet, sardines, anchovies and pickled herring on our expeditions.....all of this while reading technical manuals in 5-foot seas. When Werner reaches for the refrigerator, everyone else evacuates the cabin. The wind, rain and insects seemed a welcome relief to Werner's unique eating habits! There is no question that Werner has a cast iron stomach."

Lest you think that "Dive Boat Cuisine" is an oxymoron, read on:

STEVE LEWIS' **Voodoo Onion Hummus** .... page 10

PAUL HUMANN's **Mango Manor Salsa** .... page 12

RYAN LEBLANC's **Isle Royale Dip** .... page 14

JERI & CHUCK FELTNER's **Tuna Surprise** .... page 16

GARY GENTILE's **Open Water Banana Split** .... page 18

BILL STEINBORN's **Flavor Craver Shrimp Dip** .... page 20

Steve Lewis'
Voodoo Onion Hummus

"Getting protein from vegetable sources can be hard work....this way it's fun. Hummus is a staple in just about every country with access to the Mediterranean, and is a staple for many vegetarians. I can't actually remember life before Hummus, although it's a fact that the stuff my grandmother served me after school tasted like wallpaper paste mixed with burnt juniper bark. Hey, don't worry. This is a different recipe and produces a superior tasting dip that'll wake your tastebuds after the tedium of a long hang at 15 feet sucking on an oxygen regulator. Make it, try it, but be careful not to breathe on anyone who might be a vampire...." -- Steve Lewis

Ingredients

1 cup dried chickpeas picked over and rinsed well (you can used canned, but hear me out...and look in the instructions for the secret reason to go to the extra bother of dry.)

1 small onion, peeled and stuck with 2 whole cloves (this is the Voodoo Onion)

1 teaspoon of cumin seeds

1/2 teaspoon of coriander seeds

1 tablespoon of sesame seeds

1/4 cup fresh lemon juice

3 tablespoons of tahini (tahini is to sesame seeds as smooth peanut butter is to peanuts and is available at health food and Middle Eastern grocery stores)

3 cloves garlic, crushed and chopped (yes, I do like garlic. Use less if you have a date after the dive)

A sprinkle of sea salt

2 or 3 pinches of cayenne pepper

2 tablespoons of extra virgin olive oil (there is no substitute for good oil and this recipe is null and voil if you decide to use anything but)

1/2 cup finely chopped cilantro

Lemon zest (how do you measure this stuff?)

Instructions

Put the chickpeas in a saucepan, cover with cool water so that they are sitting under at least 2 to 3 inches of water. Let these guys soak overnight. In the morning, throw out floaters and peas that look off-color. Add enough water to cover the remainder by an inch or so, throw in the Voodoo Onion and put onto the stove. Bring to a boil and then reduce the heat, simmer and cover partly. Let cook until the peas are very tender. You may have to add more water, but resist the temptation to drown the little beggars completely. This will take more than an hour. Important point here, DO NOT add salt to the peas at this stage.

While this is going on, take your skillet and toast the cumin and coriander seeds until their perfume rises, but be careful not to char them. A couple of minutes ought to do the trick. Transfer them to a mortar and smoosh. Add the sesame seeds to the skillet and toast them on a low heat until they turn from Minnesota pale to Florida gold. Add them to the mortar and crush.

Once the chickpeas are cooked (the onion will have lost the will to retain its shape at this point), drain them, keeping the liquid for the processing step that's coming up soon. Pour the peas and what remains of the onion in the food processor. It's OK to let some cooking water get in there, too. Now in a small bowl, mix together the lemon juice, tahini, garlic, sea salt, a pinch of cayenne, the seeds and a couple of tablespoons of the cooking liquid saved from the peas.

Turn on the food processor and as it wins the argument over who's boss with the chickpeas and onion (this may take a while), add the lemon, tahini, garlic and friends mixture a tablespoon at a time. Keep the blender going until everything is pureed. Add more water as necessary. The final hummus should be light, fluffy and not too goopy. Season with more salt and cayenne to taste. Transfer the finished hummus to a sealable bowl. Sprinkle the cilantro and olive oil on top. Seal and chill.

Before serving, complete decompression obligation. Surface. Climb back on boat. remove and stow gear. Walk over to cooler and nonchalantly remove bowl of hummus and package of flatbread. (The traditional way to eat this stuff is with warm pita which might be a hard find on a dive boat. Really fresh wholewheat pita is good, but almost any fresh bread will do). Sit somewhere quiet and begin eating. Share with close friends or charge to help pay for all that helium and oxygen you just sucked back on the dive.

*You can really impress your friends with this one. This great-tasting dip takes some effort to make, but is worth the trouble. What a sense of accomplishment you'll have at the end! Warning: this will forever spoil store-bought hummus for you.

Steve Lewis discovered diving and cooking at about the same time....scuba tanks were made from stone and fire had just been discovered. Today he is an avid diver, with a particular interest in shooting video of the wooden and steel wrecks lying on the bottom of the Great Lakes.

He has logged more than 1200 decompression dives and 500 trimix dives on wrecks from Scapa Flow to Brazil. He is also an active dive instructor and guide, and has concentrated on teaching technical diving in Canada and the USA since 1994.

Steve says his major accomplishment is that he's helped convince scores of divers to have fun, stay safe, and eat well!

Photo submitted by Steve Lewis.

Paul Humann's
Mango Manor Salsa

"When not diving and taking pictures, my hobbies are gardening and cooking. Several years ago, I started collecting species of palm trees. The collection quickly outgrew my small city property. This prompted me to buy a new home on a two-acre property where I now have over 250 species of palms and cycads. On the property were 10 producing mango trees. My partner and his wife, Ned and Anna DeLoach (see page 34), jokingly called the property 'Mango Manor' and the name stuck. Come harvest season, I had to figure out what to do with all those mangos. I use the mangos in many recipes from mango pie to mango daiquiris, but my favorite is my own 'Mango Manor Salsa.'" -- Paul Humann

Ingredients and Instructions (combined)

2 fresh limes -- juice

1/2 cup olive oil (extra virgin, first cold press)

1/2 cup honey

1/2 teaspoon salt

Mix above well and pour over the following:

10 cups mango -- peeled and diced

2 bunches fresh cilantro -- finely chopped

1 large red pepper -- diced

15 fresh jalapenos -- seeded and diced (best done in a blender) and wear protective gloves

3 bunches of green/spring onions -- chopped, including most of green stems

4 celery stalks -- finely diced

Mix and refrigerate for at least one hour -- best overnight

Makes enough for about 12 hungry salsa eaters -- saves in refrigerator for about a week and can be frozen (although thawed version is not quite as good as the fresh).

*The faint-hearted may want to add the jalapenos little by little, tasting as they go. This salsa is not just fabulous to eat but colorful on the plate. An absolute winner!

Paul Humann took his first underwater photographs in the early 1960's. By the late '60's, several of his fish portraits were published in *Skin Diver's* memorable "Fish of the Month" series. His hobby became a way of life in 1970 when he left a successful law practice in Kansas to become captain/owner of the M/V *Cayman Diver,* the Caribbean's first live-aboard dive cruiser. His next eight years were spent documenting the biological diversity of the Caribbean's coral reefs.

His desire to learn and teach about sea life has been the catalyst for numerous magazine articles, four large-format photographic books and the award-winning REEF SET -- a comprehensive three-volume visual identification guide to the marine life of Florida, the Bahamas and the Caribbean. The now-famous marine life trilogy includes *Reef Fish, Reef Creatures,* and *Reef Coral Identification.* A fourth visual identification marine life guide, *Reef Fish Identification -- Galapagos,* was published in 1993, *Snorkeling Guide to Marine Life* appeared in 1995, and his most recent publication, *Coastal Fish Identification -- California to Alaska,* became available in 1996.

This pioneering work, establishing visual identification criteria for marine creatures, requires much more than the difficult task of capturing each species on film. Long hours of

observation, documentation, cataloguing and corresponding with dozens of marine taxonomists are each an essential step in the long process. In many instances, picture/voucher specimen collection was required to make positive species identifications. The specimens from these efforts now reside in the Smithsonian's National History Museum collections. Thanks to his efforts, it is now possible for underwater naturalists to make valid non-impact biodiversity assessments of reef ecosystems. His concern for the welfare of sea life has also led him to the founding of the Reef Environmental Education Foundation (REEF) -- an organization of recreational divers and snorkelers who regularly monitor marine fish populations.

Paul resides in Florida when he is not traveling the world with cameras and dive gear in tow.

Ryan LeBlanc's
Isle Royale Dip

"Back in May of 1987, I was diagnosed as having tennosynovitis in my right hand which could only be repaired by surgery. Because of my lengthy convalescence, I could not return to work and was bored out of my mind. I was delighted when Gerry Buchanan called early in June asking me if I was interested in joining him on a trip to Isle Royale to look for a sunken schooner. Gerry made my decision very easy when he mentioned he was bringing along his latest acquisitions -- 3 Farallon underwater scooters to assist in the search. How often do you get a chance to go on a mission with one of the true pioneers of tech-diving on

Lake Superior? I made a quick determination that the water therapy would do me a world of good, so I agreed to join the expedition. Accompanying us on the venture was Rick Oldale of Thunder Bay, a long-time diver and shipwreck hunter.

"We arrived at Rock Harbor on June 4, 1987, and were amazed to see we were the only vessel using this marvelous facility. The next day saw us anchored off the north end of Isle Royale in calm seas. Rick and I entered the water and searched for miles in the crystal-clear water. It was such an unbelievable sensation to be 'flying' along the ledges of Isle Royale's formidable shoals. With the scooters, we were able to catch up to lake trout in their futile attempts to evade the strange aliens who were invading their pristine space. The dives were unbelievably exquisite, but we failed to locate the elusive schooner.

"We returned to Rock Harbor that evening and noticed an eerie calm in the air. Glancing to the west, we could see the tell-tale signs of an impending squall. Within minutes, the still air was invaded by a force of biblical proportions. A huge gale swept across the harbor and buffeted our boat, *Madeline Goodrush*, which luckily was well-secured to the dock. The storm took less than a minute to pass, but impressed us with its savage force. Rick was able to catch the fury on videotape. While viewing the tape in the *Goodrush* after the tempest, Rick started to prepare something in the galley. When I asked him what he was making, he replied, 'Salsa and beans.' My response was, 'Yeah, right.' He retorted, 'Don't knock it until you try it.' I have made this recipe on several occasions since. Whenever I prepare it for someone for the first time, their usual response is, 'Yeah, right.' Ultimately, everyone who

has tried it is amazed by its simplicity and how good it tastes. It does not require a stove or oven and can be prepared in seconds. Therefore it is an ideal recipe for boaters and divers."
-- Ryan LeBlanc

Ryan leans on a mast from the deep *Gunilda* in the town of Rossport, Ontario.

Ingredients

1 can of pork and beans

1/2 jar of salsa

1 bag of tortilla chips

Instructions

Combine one cold can of pork and beans in a bowl with half a jar of salsa. Mix thoroughly. Use tortilla chips as "dippers." Enjoy.

*Make this for your friends and let the ingredients be a secret. They don't have to know that something this good could also be so easy!

Ryan LeBlanc is recognized as the Father of Diving on the North Shore of Lake Superior. He holds three Dive Instructor Certifications and has served on the Executive Committee of Save Ontario shipwrecks and as Northwest Regional Director of the Ontario Underwater Council. Some notable achievements in his diving career have included working with the Cousteau team aboard the *Calypso* as well as doing many air and mixed gas dives from 1979 to 1981 on one of the Great Lakes' most famous shipwrecks: the *Gunilda* in 254 feet of water.

Ryan LeBlanc stands beside the huge boiler, originally hidden by a blanket of debris, marking the site of the 1899 shipwreck *Ontario* which he located in 1977 off remote Battle Island in northern Lake Superior. Joyce Hayward [see p. 30] sits on top.

Ryan's passion for shipwreck research has led to the discovery of many northern Lake Superor shipwrecks. His most recent discovery took place in the summer of 2001 when his team located the long fabled "Graveyard of Ships" in Thunder Bay Harbor where 30 vessels were found in a half mile square in 250 feet of water.

Jeri & Chuck Feltner's
Tuna Surprise

"After a dive back in the late 1970's in the Straits of Mackinac, Chuck and I were cruising under the Mackinac Bridge and encountered another boat of divers which included Norm Wilkes, Ray Dickerson, George Dunkelberg and Rose Armstrong. We tied our boats together and told dive war stories as we drifted through the Straits. At one point, I decided to surprise everyone with something to nibble on -- thus, the Tuna Surprise!" -- Jeri Baron Feltner

Ingredients

1   6 1/2 oz. can of tuna, drained

3 tablespoons mayonnaise

1/2 teaspoon paprika

1/8 teaspoon pepper

1/8 teaspoon garlic powder

2 tablespoons sweet pepper relish

2 tablespoons sliced green onion

Instructions

Mix together,

serve on crackers

and enjoy the people.

What a nice treat after diving in the cool, fresh waters of the Great Lakes!

Chuck Feltner was born in North Carolina and earned a Ph.D. degree in Engineering from the University of Illinois. As a boy, Chuck lived on the Outer Banks, a strand of islands off the coast of North Carolina that is strewn with shipwrecks. A PADI Divemaster, he has searched for, found, and documented numerous wrecks around the Great Lakes. He served as the first Public Member-at-Large on Michigan's Underwater Salvage Committee.

Dr. Feltner is widely known in the midwest marine historical and scuba diving communities for his published articles and presentations on shipwrecks, and courses on "How to Research Great Lakes Shipwrecks." He is a co-founder, and was chairman for the first five years, of the Great Lakes Shipwreck Festival, an annual event held in Dearborn, Michigan. After retiring from the Ford Motor Company, he began a consulting firm.

Jeri Baron Feltner was born and raised in Michigan. An enthusiastic PADI Divemaster, she has produced underwater films of the wrecks of the propeller *Eber Ward* and the brig *Sandusky* which received acclaim at underwater shows in Chicago, Detroit and Toronto.

Jeri is co-author with her husband of two books, *Great Lakes Maritime History: Bibliography and Sources of Information* and *Shipwrecks of the Straits of Mackinac.* She was

Editor from 1980 to 1982 of *Diving Times,* a midwest newspaper on scuba diving. Ms. Feltner worked several years in the ski travel business and for the Ford Motor Company. She is presently very actively involved in efforts to save and restore the lighthouse at DeTour, Michigan.

The Feltners divide their time living in the Detroit area and in a residence set in the wilderness of Drummond Island in northern Lake Huron.

Gary Gentile's
Open Water Banana Split

"One thing we always carry on a dive boat is bananas because we have a thing called the Banana Peel Test. This is a determination for establishing whether the current is too strong to dive in. I developed this procedure on the *Empress of Ireland* [Canada's worst maritime disaster, this wreck lies in the St. Lawrence River in the province of Quebec] where there are very strong tides....When you have an outgoing tide, which goes along with the flow of the river, it could be severe, so severe that you literally cannot make it to the anchor line. So, in order to save ourselves from having to get all dressed and ready to go when the tide looks like it might be strong, I use the Banana Peel Test.

" I peel the banana, eat the banana, and then take the banana peel up to the bow. I throw the peel in the water and I immediately run as fast as I can along the boat, over the gear, to the stern. If the banana peel beats me to the stern of the boat, then the current is running too strong to dive....

Tom Farnquist, left [check out his recipe on page 32], helps prepare Gary Gentile for a deep shipwreck dive in Lake Superior. Those are whitecaps in the background, not bananas.

"Most of the time, I get my bananas in the store, but one time we had a situation diving in the ocean in which I came up from a dive, and I was about a hundred feet from the dive boat, and people on the boat were waving their arms and pointing to me in the water. Naturally, I thought there was a shark, so I started looking around and instead, a bunch of bananas floated past me. And so I grabbed this bunch of bananas and naturally I had a mesh bag with me, and so I stuffed the bananas in the bag and then they started pointing at other bananas, and I ended up recovering quite a few bunches of bananas, as did everyone else on the boat. Apparently it was a deck cargo that got washed overboard in a storm and all these bananas were littering the surface of the sea, and I recovered enough bananas that I was able to eat bananas for at least a month, one or two a day. I was really banana-ed out by the end of that. By the way, bananas are impervious to seawater, they're waterproof because of the peel, so they were not damaged in any way, and they were green to begin with, so they had a lot of ripening to do.

"Ironically, a few years later, I was on another boat with two of the same people who were on the banana trip, and we saw, in the distance, an ocean liner, and as we were traveling from one wreck site to another, we saw two five-gallon buckets floating in the water. So the captain veered his boat around and the wash of the boat turned them upside-down and they were buckets of ice cream. We assumed that they had been thrown overboard by the waiters on the cruise liner because they had melted on the outside, and they couldn't refreeze them, and this was like their afternoon buffet, and so we circled around and we got crab nets and we scooped up these two five-gallon chunks of ice cream, put them in buckets on the boat. Then we proceeded to eat the ice cream. The saltwater had gotten into the ice cream, but only on the outside, so we just scraped off the outside with our hands and then just stuck our hands inside this frozen ice cream on the middle and took out big chunks of it and ate ice-cold ice cream, which, on a dive boat, was a rarity because dive boats in those days did not have refrigerators or freezers or microwave ovens or any of that stuff. The 3 of us who had been on the previous trip reminisced about that and thought how ironic it would have been if we could have had both situations occur on the same day because then we could have had banana splits." -- Gary Gentile

Boy! Some people will eat anything that washes up on shore or floats by the dive boat!

Gary Gentile became an avid wreck diver shortly after beginning his diving career in 1970. By 1974, he was exploring the *Andrea Doria* and has since made over 200 dives to this famous shipwreck. Other challenging dives he has made are to the *Lusitania,* in 300 feet off Ireland, and to the *Monitor* off North Carolina after winning a lengthy legal battle with NOAA for the right to dive there. Gary is a noted authority on shipwreck research, artifact recovery and preservation techniques, and has compiled an extensive library of books, photographs, drawings, plans, and original source materials on ships and shipwrecks. He is the author of several books, most of them about East Coast shipwrecks, and scores of articles. Many of his photographs have been published in books, periodicals, newspapers, brochures, advertisements, corporate reports, museum displays, postcards, film and television. He lectures extensively on wilderness and underwater topics, and conducts seminars on advanced wreck-diving techniques and high-tech diving equipment.

Bill Steinborn's
Flavor Craver Shrimp Dip

"We got this recipe from another diver's wife when she used to make it during our cookouts up in Door County, Wisconsin, in the early 1970's -- during our wreck diving trips, of course." -- Bill Steinborn

Ingredients

1/2 cup Heinz Chili Sauce

1 package (8 oz.) softened cream cheese

1/2 cup mayonnaise or slaw dressing

2 teaspoons horseradish

1/4 cup chopped onion

1 can (4 1/2 oz.) tiny shrimp (deveined), rinsed and drained

Instructions

Blend chili sauce gradually into cream cheese. Mix in mayonnaise, onion and horseradish. Fold in shrimp. Cover and chill at least 1 hour for best flavor. Makes 2 1/2 cups.

*This is a nice tangy dip. It's so good, in fact, it even makes a great open-face sandwich.

Bill Steinborn started snorkeling in about 1955 and turned to scuba in 1961. He notes that 1967 was the year of his "first good wreck dive." He is a Founding Member of the Rockford (IL) Divers Association. For five years, he served on the Executive Board of the Illinois Council of Skin and Scuba Divers, including terms as President from 1975 to 1978. From 1975 to 1985, he was a speaker, emcee and Room Chairman for the "Our World--Underwater" Show in Chicago, and served as Vice President (Exhibits) of the same show from 1975 to 1998, and as President of the OW-U Scholarship Society in 1993-1994. He wrote abut a dozen articles on Great Lakes diving for *Skin Diver* magazine between 1980 and 1991.

Bill Steinborn (right) appeared in Jack McKenney's DEMA film "Scuba Dive America" in 1986. He is seen here with Jack McKenney (left) and the cinematographer's son, John, who today is a successful underwater filmmaker following in his late father's footsteps. Submitted by Bill Steinborn.

SECOND COURSE: SOUPS, SALADS, SANDWICHES

What does a world record-holder in deep diving eat before and after a dive? The answer, of course, is: anything he wants. In Jim Bowden's case, his favorite pre-dive food is arroz con leche, similar to a sweet rice pudding. After the dive, his favorite re-charge is Caldo de pollo -- good old Mexican chicken soup with a healthy squeeze of lime juice. Oxygen on the side? [See page 110 for one of Jim's favorite recipes when he's at home in Texas.]

Soups, salads, and sandwiches do not need to be boring. Try these from our scuba chefs:

BERNIE CHOWDHURY's **Moon Chowder** .... page 22

ART BACHRACH's **Hot Lips Soup with Shrimp & Pork** .... page 24

ADAM RAVETCH's **Chunky Natsiq Soup** .... page 26

PATRICK HAMMER's **Key West Clam Chowder** .... page 28

JOYCE HAYWARD's **New England Clam Chowder** .... page 30

TOM FARNQUIST's **Whitefish Pt. Whitefish Chowder** .... page 32

NED & ANNA DELOACH's **Bimini Slaw** .... page 34

CRIS KOHL's **Slaw** .... page 36

ZALE PARRY's **Diver's Delight Cucumbers** .... page 38

BILL HAMILTON's **World Class Tomato Sandwich** .... page 40

BRIAN SKERRY's **Survival Grilled Cheese Sandwich** .... page 42

GARY CHESNUT's **Savory Salmon Sandwich** .... page 44

Bernie Chowdhury's
Moon Chowder

"This dish is for people who enjoy spicy and tingly food. We enjoy spicy food, Diana is a wonderful cook and we have fun creating new recipes. The traditional way to eat a soup like this within the family is without straining or removing anything from the pot. We eat it all, leaving nothing but the bones! We thought Moon Chowder was a romantic name for a soup that is a great favorite of ours." -- Bernie Chowdhury

Left: Bernie and his wife Diana, the Dish of his Life.

Ingredients (For 6 people)

7 cups of water

1/2 chicken with bones, cut up

3 potatoes, diced

1 red onion, diced

3 bay leaves

1/2 jalapeno pepper, seeded and cut into small pieces

1 stick of celery, diced

1 lime, cut into quarters

2 carrots, diced

1 tablespoon salt

3 slices of ginger

1 cube of chicken stock

3 cloves of garlic, minced or crushed in a garlic press (use all of it)

1 red pepper, cut into strips

1 cup parsley, chopped

Instructions

Into a large pot with the water boiling, add the chicken, potatoes, onion, carrots, celery, jalapeno pepper, bay leaves, ginger, salt, lime, garlic and chicken stock.

Lower the heat and cover.

Let it simmer for 1 1/2 hours.

Add the red pepper and let it simmer for 20 minutes.

When the Moon Chowder is ready, serve with chopped parsley on top.

This soup is good and "tingly" as promised. The colors in the bowl - with the green of the parsley and the red of the peppers - make it look as good as it tastes.

Bernie Chowdhury has been a NAUI/PADI open water instructor since 1988. He has led trips to the Andrea Doria, to Scapa Flow in Scotland, and to Narvik, Norway. His diving "firsts" include the *H.M.S. Pheasant* at 280 feet, the *H.M.S. Hampshire* at 210 feet, the German World War II wreck, *Blucher,* at 300+ feet, and preliminary explorations of several underwater caves in Iceland.

He has published articles on wreck and cave diving, and he is the founder and publisher of *IMMERSED,* the international technical diving magazine.

Bernie's book, *The Last Dive,* was published in North America by Harper Collins in late 2000 and has received critical acclaim and been translated into several languages.

Bernie has made presentations about cave diving in Iceland, various shipwreck experiences he has had, and the lessons learned from *The Last Dive* at a large variety of venues, including many of the major Scuba Shows.

He is a Fellow of the Explorer's Club.

Art Bachrach's
Hot Lips Soup with Shrimp and Pork

" In my career, I have had the opportunity to live and work in a variety of climes and in each area, I have learned from the regional cuisine. I spent many years at the University of Virginia, as a graduate student and then medical faculty following my PhD. Virginia has a rich (I mean rich!) cuisine and the main recipe I drew from my days there was Mr. Jefferson's recipe for Holiday Egg Nog.

"Living in Arizona taught me the flavors of the Southwest and Mexico and, especially, learning to do a mean ceviche on Mexican dive boats. Off Guaymas, we took jars of Jalapenos, tomatoes, chiles, et cetera, and someone speared a fish or two. Voila! Ceviche after a couple of hours. But Arizona Southwest cuisine pales in the light of New Mexican food, New Mexico being the area of high mountains and desert to which I retired after being at the Naval Medical Research Institute in Maryland for 18 years.

With colleague Glen Egstrom (left). See Glen's recipe on page 70.

"Maryland taught me the real crab cake and, along with Virginia, the joy of oysters. At one Underwater Canada Show, Glen [Egstrom] and I came up with a fantastic oyster recipe -- the Vancouver area oysters were as big as potatoes! -- and we sent a batch up to the dive show staff. Later on, we found out that someone had decided to warm them and placed them in the microwave. The resulting explosion probably triggered seismographs all over.

"Diving in the Caribbean, of course, developed a love for the Island cuisine, but my favorite still remains Oriental, Korean in particular, for the wide variety of dishes and the generous use of garlic, which someone once called the ketchup of the intellectuals.

"This soup recipe came from a course I took in Maryland from a superb chef, Joan Shih, who taught us every Chinese cuisine from Cantonese (boring!) to Hakka and Hunan. The soup goes well with such dishes as Mongolian Lamb but especially well with Oriental whole fish dishes and prawns. I find that the modern techniques of freezing fish makes it possible for us even at 7,000 feet in the high desert to get good seafood, so my cooking days are not over, just tempered by the magnificent Northern New Mexican flavors." -- Art Bachrach

Ingredients

8 oz. shrimp, washed, shelled, deveined, cut into quarters

4 oz. lean pork, ground

3 10-ounce cans of chicken broth

3 cups clear water

4 Ginger root pieces, fresh

4 Cloves of garlic, peeled and crushed

3 Eggs, beaten with 1/2 teaspoon salt

Dash of black pepper

4 Green onions (scallions)

3 tablespoons soy sauce

3 tablespoons cornstarch

5 tablespoons rice vinegar

1/2 teaspoon black pepper

2 tablespoons chili sesame oil

Peanut oil for stir frying shrimp and pork

Ingredients for preparing marinade for shrimp & pork: 1/4 teaspoon salt, a dash of black pepper, 3/4 tablespoon of soy sauce, and 1 tablespoon of dry sherry.

Instructions

Mix shrimp and pork in bowl and marinate in above mix for 20 minutes at room temperature. Pour 2 tablespoons peanut oil in wok, add 2 pieces ginger and garlic to hot oil and let sizzle. Place shrimp/pork melange into the hot oil and stir fry until cooked; remove to plate.

Mix 1 teaspoon salt, 2 tablespoons soy sauce and 2 tablespoons cornstarch and 1 cup cold water, set aside.

At high heat: Put the 2 remaining ginger root slices into chicken broth and 2 cups of cold water in sauce pot and bring to a boil. Pour the shrimp/pork mixture into the boiling soup and then add the soy/cornstarch mixture. Slowly drop the eggs along long chopsticks so that they flow onto the soup surface, moving the chopsticks in a circle (letting it flower -- this is egg drop), continually stirring. Then add rice vinegar, 1/2 teaspoon black pepper and scallions to soup. Add chili sesame oil. Serve hot.

*Keep a box of tissues nearby for when your eyes water and your nose runs. But it's worth a good cry! Lip-burning hot and scrumptious!

Dr. Art Bachrach, a retired Navy scientist, is a Past President of the Undersea Medical Society and Editor of the journal, *Underwater Medicine.* He has received the prestigious Leonard Greenstone Award for contributions to Diving Safety, the Our World - Underwater Award, and the Underwater Society of America's coveted NOGI Award. He is the author of *Psychological Research: An Introduction,* and co-author (with Glen Egstrom; see page 70) of *Stress and Performance in Diving.* He is currently devoting his time to a museum exhibit and writing a book on the history of diving.

Adam Ravetch's
Chunky Natsiq Soup

Adam's Kitchen: On one of his many Arctic diving expeditions, Adam Ravetch partakes of a subsistence meal prepared by an Inuk hunter. Photo submitted by Adam Ravetch.

"While I am filming in the Arctic, in temperatures well below zero, and diving under the ice, miles from the nearest town or supermarket, there is nothing more efficient in energizing your body and keeping you warm between dives than the wild meat of the Arctic.

"'Natsiq' is Inuktutuk for 'Ringed Seal.' I partake in this delicacy only when accompanied by a professional Inuk subsistence hunter in the Arctic. Often it is a matter of survival." -- Adam Ravetch

Ingredients

1 small natsiq, skinned and gutted; separate and keep liver, heart and other organs

1 large pot of Arctic snow

2 dry packets of tomato soup

1 large onion

2 quarts of natsiq blood

3 large chunks of natsiq fat

Salt

Instructions

Must be outside in temperatures at least 15 below zero. These conditions make you very cold and very hungry fast. Natsiq can be taken only when accompanied by a professional Inuk subsistence hunter. Chunky Natsiq Soup can only be made on a naptha gas Coleman stove.

Place large pot of snow onto Coleman stove. Heat until melted. Add more snow until pot is 3/4 full and boiling.

Add choice parts of natsiq into boiling water: some ribs, a little heart, and lots of natsiq meat. Do not separate the fat from the meat. Cook it all. Now add the tomato soup packets, onions and blood. Bring to a boil. Cook until tender.

Find a piece of flat cardboard for a plate, or just kneel in the snow. Take the meat out of the pot and eat the meat first until full. Before you're done, pour the broth from the pot into a glass or mug and drink until done.

Guaranteed to bring you instant and long-lasting warmth!

*DON'T try this one at home, kids. Just read and enjoy the story!

Adam Ravetch was born and educated in California. His skills as a marine biologist, scuba diver and award-winning cinematographer have involved him in a myriad of projects and research taking him to the far corners of the earth.

During the past 15 years, Adam, a former Our World - Underwater Scholarship winner, has been prolific, first learning his trade in underwater cinematography. Adam has filmed and documented the creatures of the world's oceans for more than 90 shows, working for the Discovery Channel, NHK Japan, CBS, NBC, The Cousteau Society, and "The Last Frontier" series with John Stoneman.

Seeking a creative outlet, Adam then began producing and directing his own films and won several awards for his first short film, *Ice Puppy,* and also gained recognition for his second film, *The Next Generation.* In his pursuit of knowledge and the ultimate photographic challenge, Adam has become one of only a handful of Arctic filmmakers who dives and shoots film under the Arctic ice cap. In 1997, *Toothwalkers, Giants of the Arctic Ice,* made for PBS' "Nature," focused on walrus and showcased an array of images the likes of which few have ever seen. In stunning underwater photography, he documents the unicorn-like Narwhal, an 18-foot Greenland shark, and the first ever underwater footage of wild walrus societies.

In 2000, Adam went on to produce for National Geographic Television, *Toothed Titans,* diving deeper into the walruses' world and revealing the intimate and dramatic life of this sabertooth-like titan of the North. In this extraordinary one-hour film, a newborn walrus calf and its mother are stalked and pursued relentlessly by a hungry polar bear on the prowl. *Toothed Titans* delivers never-before-seen, dramatic natural history behaviour of these remarkable animals.

Adam's most recent accomplishment is a one-hour film for PBS' Emmy award-winning natural history series, "The Living Edens," *Arctic Oasis.* Airing in 2003 as a PBS "Nature Special," *Arctic Oasis* promises to be the modern day version of *Nanook of the North* as Adam documents a young Inuit father's quest to pass on his wisdom of the North to his young son in a harsh and frozen world.

Currently, Adam is in production on two hours of Arctic programing for National Geographic Television, *Giants of the Arctic Ice.* Simply stated, Adam is dedicated to filmmaking and bringing the unforgettable details of animals' lives and their relationships to people to the screen.

Patrick Hammer's
Key West Clam Chowder

"While in Key West, I learned about this from a girl I met at Captain Tony's Saloon. Wow! What a treat!" -- Patrick Hammer

Ingredients

4 oz. bacon, cut small

1 carrot, thinly sliced

3 celery sticks, thinly sliced

1 yellow onion, coarsely chopped

2 bay leaves

3 cloves of garlic

1 teaspoon pepper

1 teaspoon chicken bouillon

2 6-oz. cans of minced clams, undrained

1 teaspoon Worcestershire sauce

2 1/2 cups finely chopped, peeled potatoes

1/4 teaspoon dried thyme

2 cups milk

1 cup light cream

2 tablespoons all-purpose flour

Instructions

Fry bacon in large pot. Remove a few pieces for use as garnish later. Add carrot and celery, and cook over medium heat for 2 minutes. Add onion and bay leaves. Then add whole cloves of garlic. Stir and add pepper.

Fold in the clams (with juice) and let simmer.

Add potatoes, bouillon, Worcestershire sauce and thyme. Cover and simmer 10 minutes or until potatoes are tender.

Mash potatoes with fork. Combine milk, cream and flour (whisk together) and add to pot. Keep it thick.

Heat to just under the boiling point. Cook 1 to 2 minutes. Sprinkle with bacon to serve.

*Oh boy, if you think you don't like clam chowder, you will, after tasting this! If you already like it, you'll love this.

Patrick Hammer started diving in Florida about 40 years ago. He was a PADI Instructor and saw a need for a scuba store on Chicago's south side. Patrick opened his first store in 1974, and, through the years, he has opened stores all over Illinois, in Atlanta and at Crystal River, Florida. After many years of hard work, Patrick dropped down to one store, in Alsip, Illinois. After 10 years, he saw a need for a professional dive center in Orland Park, Illinois, and opened a 7,500-square-foot dive center with a beautiful pool.

Patrick is one of PADI's oldest course directors, not in age, but in years of experience. He became a PADI course director in 1975 and has conducted training since then. He currently trains instructors in Illinois, Arizona, Jamaica, St. Lucia and Bonaire. Patrick is credited in the development of over 10 PADI Distinctive specialty courses, and presently offers 35 courses.

In 1999, Patrick became President of "Our World - Underwater," the largest scuba show in the Midwest.

An Added Treat from Pat Hammer: *A Recipe for "Fresh Scuba Diver"*

Ingredients

1 basic scuba manual	2 masks
1 pool	2 pairs of fins
1 small classroom	2 snorkels
2 scuba tanks	2 weight belts
2 BCD's	1 nice open water site
2 regulators	

Instructions

Start with mixing in my knowledge with the new diver's basic swim skills, simmer for a while in the shallow water and, as competency builds, move the diver to the classroom and mix in some humor, fun and knowledge. "Expand on what they read."

Administer a final test and take the blend to a beautiful freshwater pond.

Stir in a fun weekend in the country, mixed with other divers and let sit for 30 to 40 minutes at 30 feet. On day two, repeat.

You now have a scuba diver.

Joyce Hayward's
New England Clam Chowder

"This recipe has been handed down through several generations of the Stewart [Joyce's maiden name] family who settled along the New England coast beginning in the early 1800's. This recipe was handed down to me prior to the popularity of skimmed 2% milk and prepared for me as a child with whole milk. The cream was not removed from the top of the bottle but rather used in the chowder to provide a creamy texture. The potatoes were never so soft that they fell apart in the chowder but were never hard. Selecting just the right potatoes and cooking them to the correct texture was the most difficult part of the recipe for me!"
-- Joyce Hayward

Ingredients

2-3 slices salt pork (1/4 - 3/8 inches thick)

1 cup diced clams (substitute 1 can)

2 onions (about 2 1/2" diameter each)

2 medium potatoes

4 cups of milk (2 more if you like it thin)

(no salt or butter to be used)

Instructions

Cut pork into strips 3/8 inch wide and then dice into 3/8 inch cubes.

Cut onions into slices 1/4 inch thick and dice.

Cut potatoes into 1/4 inch slices, cutting these into 3/8 inch strips and dice into 3/8 inch cubes.

Put the pork into 2-3 qt. kettle and toast it to a golden brown. Remove pork when light brown (note: keep turning the cubes over to brown on all sides). The diced potatoes should be cooking separately in boiling water while you fry the onions. Ten minutes should do. The milk should also be heating while you cook the onions and potatoes. Be careful not to let the milk come to a boil!

Add onions to fat and bring to a light brown. Add diced clams and heat for about 3 minutes.

When the clams have heated 3 minutes, add the cooked potatoes (drained of water) and add the hot milk. Continue to heat for 3-4 minutes, and then turn off the heat.

The chowder will have better flavor if prepared the day before you eat it, and allowed to "age." Be sure you let the chowder cool down before you chill it by putting it in your refrigerator. When you put it in the refrigerator, leave it uncovered for at least one hour.

Do not cover the kettle when cooking nor when cooling. Chowder will sour if cooled when covered.

Serving: Once again, be careful not to boil the chowder when heating to serve the second day. Serve with chowder crackers and the browned pork cubes on the side. (Pork cubes will be dry, small from shrinking after the frying, and will be somewhat crispy when first dropped on the served chowder).

Joyce hangs off after a deep dive inside the wreck of the steamer, *Vienna,* in 148' of Lake Superior water.

Forget your cholesterol and enjoy the salt pork "croutons" -- it's a delicious touch for this lovely, delicately flavored chowder.

Joyce Hayward, the "Lady of the Lakes," has served as an officer in national, regional and Canadian organizations and was appointed by the governor of Ohio to advise shipwreck management in that state. She does underwater photography, creating and presenting multi-projector programs at major conventions where she is frequently the only woman shipwreck speaker, and her underwater photography has appeared in various publications. Joyce also organizes courses in underwater archaeology. She was featured on a PBS special, "The Great Lakes In Depth," for her work in shipwreck and marine biology education. Joyce started diving in 1982 and has been involved in deep (over 160 feet) diving, including tri-mix, for several years. She was inducted into the Women Divers Hall of Fame in 2001.

Tom Farnquist's
Whitefish Point Whitefish Chowder

"My early interest in scuba diving and exploring shipwrecks lead to an introduction to noted wreck hunter John Steele in 1972. I was asked to participate in an expedition organized by Mr. Steele to search for and document shipwrecks in an area of eastern Lake Superior ominously known to sailors as 'Lake Superior's Shipwreck Coast,' which extends west from Whitefish Point 80 miles to Munising, Michigan. Of the 550 shipwrecks hidden beneath Superior's treacherous waters, 200 are known to be lost in this area.

"Lake Superior can be a bountiful provider as well as a ruthless tyrant. Her unpredictable mood swings often prevented departure or forced you to seek the relative safety of the Whitefish Point Harbor of Refuge. Mountainous seas whipped up by the prevailing winds of the season or the sudden onset of summertime fog can develop with little warning. During these forced delays, friendships developed with local commercial fishermen and area residents who often shared not only tales of adventure and shipwrecks, but the many recipes for preparing whitefish and lake trout handed down over the centuries.

"Brown's Fishery, located within the secure confines of the harbor, had the reputation for delivering the finest quality fresh fish available on the Great Lakes. Caught in the cold, deep waters off the Point, these catches are enjoyed in many restaurants throughout the Midwest. Many hours were spent in Brown's fish house talking to employees who cleaned and prepared fish for delivery or drop-in sales. I can't imagine the thousands of fish that Tom Brown Sr. and Tom Brown Jr. processed over the many years their families operated before closing the business recently. Often, Tom Jr., better known as Buddy, would offer samples of fish he would be cooking in the back room. I was introduced to many different ways of preparing fish, all very good. This recipe captures the essence of the rugged nature of the fishermen who made a living in the often treacherous waters off Whitefish Point." -- Tom Farnquist

Ingredients

4 strips of bacon - diced	1 teaspoon celery salt
1 large onion - chopped	1 teaspoon salt
2-3 leeks or green onions - sliced	1/2 teaspoon pepper
3-4 potatoes - diced	2 cups milk or cream
1 can of chicken broth (14 1/2 oz.)	3/4 to 1 lb. whitefish - deboned, without skin
1 cup water	- cut into chunks

Instructions

Brown bacon until partly crisp. Add onions and leeks. Sauté slowly until tender, but not brown. Add potatoes, broth, water and seasoning. Cover and simmer 20-30 minutes until potatoes are nearly done. Add pieces of whitefish and simmer until fish is done (about 10-15 minutes). Add milk or cream and heat (do not boil). Serve with a pat of butter and garnish with a sprig of parsley. Serves 4-6.

*This is a delicious, hearty soup to warm the bones on a cold day.

Tom Farnquist worked as a junior high school teacher from 1968 until 1991, when he turned his full attention to Whitefish Point, Michigan. He founded and established the Great Lakes Shipwreck Museum, arguably the most successful maritime museum in the Midwest, in the restored Whitefish Point Lightstation. Since Tom became Executive Director of the Great Lakes Shipwreck Historical Society (which he founded in 1978) in nearby Sault Ste. Marie, Michigan, in 1985 (a position which he still holds today), he has been responsible for raising nearly $2,000,000 in private, corporate and government funding for the museum.

Tom taught scuba at Lake Superior State University from 1975 to 1980. An accomplished underwater photographer specializing in 16mm film and video, Tom received his Rebreather - Advanced Technical Diving Certification in 1997.

He organized and directed three diving expeditions to the wreck of the *Edmund Fitzgerald*, in 1989, 1994 and 1995. Working directly with families of the lost crewmen, the Canadian Navy, National Geographic Society and other organizations, he directed the recovery of the *Edmund Fitzgerald's* bell in 1995, with his article on that project appearing in *National Geographic Magazine* in January, 1996. His numerous awards include two Emmys for his 1989 and 1995 films on Lake Superior shipwrecks.

Tom Farnquist and the bell from the nearby wreck of the *Edmund Fitzgerald*, the Great Lakes' most famous shipwreck which sank in 529' of water with all 29 hands in a severe storm in late 1975 only a few miles from the Shipwreck Museum at Whitefish Point. Photo taken and submitted by Chris Winters.

Ned & Anna DeLoach's
Bimini Slaw

"We lived in Bimini [in the Bahamas] a good part of the five years that we worked on the reef fish behaviour book. Keeping fresh vegetables was a challenge, so we had 101 ways to prepare cabbage. This was one of our favorites, passed on to us by dear friend Phoebe Foster and dubbed 'Bimini Slaw' by one of our kids." -- Ned and Anna DeLoach

Ingredients (serves 6)

1/2 medium cabbage, chopped

1 package Ramen noodles (we like Oriental flavor)

2 or 3 ounces sliced, toasted almonds

1/2 cup salad oil

3 tablespoons vinegar

3 tablespoons sugar

1 tablespoon chopped onion

Instructions

Dressing: In a blender, mix seasoning packet from Ramen noodles with vinegar, oil, sugar and onion. Set aside.

Boil the Ramen noodles for 3 minutes, rinse in cold water and drain.

Toss the chopped cabbage, noodles, almonds and dressing.

The bright, fresh taste of this slaw will make you forget ordinary cole slaw. Don't expect leftovers!

Ned DeLoach is the author of *The Diving Guide to Underwater Florida* (in all its 10 increasingly-larger editions since 1977!) and *Reef Fish Behaviour: Florida, Bahamas and Caribbean* with partner Paul Humann [see page 12].

Ned first visited Florida with his parents on a family vacation in the mid-1950's and, seeing three barefoot boys edging their way down an embankment to the waterfront with masks and fins in hand, decided that he wanted to try that. After receiving his first set of flippers and a mask for Christmas that year, he explored the bottom of every swimming pool he could find in the region where he lived in western Texas. After school in 1969, he moved to Florida where he worked as a teacher, spending his summers diving. His strong desire to share his findings with other divers prompted him to publish his first guide in June, 1972 -- the 48-page *Diving and Recreational Guide to Florida Springs*. A year later, his 66-page *Diving Guide to the Florida Keys* appeared. In 1977, he combined the two books with expanded information to include Florida's East and West Coasts, and thus the first edition of *Ned DeLoach's Diving Guide to Underwater Florida* was born.

Anna DeLoach serves as videographer and spotter on their photographic expeditions. She is co-owner of The Cake Shop of San Jose (www.jaxcakeshop.com) where she spends her time designing custom wedding and special occasion cakes.

They both love to cook, and they share the kitchen duties at home.

Cris Kohl's
Slaw

Cris in the mid-1980's with one of his early scuba diving trophies.

"I spent the winter of '88 in Australia, driving around the country in an old, beat-up stationwagon and shooting pictures in the waters of the Great Barrier Reef and the Indian Ocean near Perth. I figured that if it's winter in Canada, it must be summer Down Under, so I was pretty proud of my timing. WRONG! January to April plague Australia with the windiest weather for scuba diving, so I got blown off a lot of divesites, including the fabled *Yongala* shipwreck twice! In fact, a violent quirk of nature which the Aussies affectionately named 'Cyclone Charlie' forced me to remain in the east coast town of MacKay for three days because police had closed the road north to Townsville due to severe flooding. I had picked up a hitchhiker earlier that day outside Rockhampton, and the two of us rented a furnished trailer, steel cables holding it down to long stakes driven deeply into the ground, in MacKay for 20 Australian dollars a night. The only store we could reach through the incessant torrential downpour and strong winds sold us good Australian beer and the basic ingredients for an emergency coleslaw.

"Several years later, when I began dating Joan Forsberg, the meal she made for me when I first visited her at her place included an 'improved' version of my Aussie slaw concoction which I had told her about. She fixed it so impressively that I simply had to marry the girl. Here's that improved version!" -- Cris Kohl

Ingredients

1/2 large head green cabbage, shredded

1/2 small head red cabbage, shredded

1 carrot, grated

1 zucchini, unpeeled, seeds removed, grated

1 cup parsley, chopped

1/2 to 1 envelope Ranch dressing powder mix, to taste

1 cup mayonnaise

1/2 cup sunflower kernels

Instructions

Mix the vegetables and 1/2 envelope Ranch dressing powder together with your hands in a huge bowl. Enjoy the colors in the mixture. Add the mayonnaise. Continue to mix with your hands. This part gets messy, but it's good to be really in touch with your food.

Add the sunflower kernels and make sure everything is thoroughly mixed together -- no stray, left-out, dry cabbage hiding at the bottom of the bowl. You will notice it loses a lot of volume as the mayonnaise is mixed in.

Chill and serve. Tell everyone to kiss the cook.

*A food processor makes short work of the shredding and grating chores, and prevents grated knuckles. The first day, the salad is crispier and stronger-flavored than the next day when it mellows out a bit.

Cris Kohl, from Windsor, Ontario, and now of Chicago, intrigued by shipwrecks after visiting Bermuda and the Florida Keys in 1974 (and with the underwater world in general after discovering the joys of snorkeling in the Mediterranean Sea off the Spanish town of Almunecar in 1972) began exploring Great Lakes waters. With an English degree plus a Master's degree in History, he wrote nine books beginning in 1985, including the popular *Dive Ontario!* guides, the best-selling two-volume set called *The 100 Best Great Lakes Shipwrecks*, and the acclaimed *The Great Lakes Diving Guide,* as well as hundreds of magazine and newsletter articles over the past 20 years promoting these incredible freshwater wrecks. A certified Divemaster and Full Cave Diver, his intense research, prize-winning underwater photography, vigor and sense of drama have made him a popular speaker at major scuba shows and maritime history conferences.

He has spent the majority of his life around water, whether crossing the Atlantic Ocean by ship five times or exploring his beloved Great Lakes in his sailboat or powerboat, living on board for weeks at a time. He has explored and photographed hundreds of shipwrecks in three oceans and all five Great Lakes, and has had his work published in major scuba magazines *(Sport Diver, Skin Diver, Immersed, Discover Diving, Diver Magazine* and others) and newspapers such as the *Washington Post* and the *Toronto Globe and Mail.*

Cris is on the Executive Board of the Underwater Archaeological Society of Chicago.

He is married to writer, historian and dive buddy Joan Forsberg. They both have history degrees, a lifelong love of ships and a fascination with researching and exploring shipwrecks.

Cris Kohl was recently on board a tugboat in the harbor of Duluth, Minnesota, at the extreme western end of Lake Superior. Photo by Chet Childs, President, Underwater Archaeological Society of Chicago.

Zale Parry's
Diver's Delight Cucumbers

"This is the only way I'll eat cucumbers...a treat from my mother's kitchen a gillion years ago. I grew up on a lake in Wisconsin. My daddy loved fishing the perch, bass and Walleye pike. We were served fried, baked, boiled (as in soup) and pickled (as in preserved) fish. When in season, the cucumbers were a special delight with the Sunday dinner." -- Zale Parry

Right: Zale Parry using Northill Airlung, October, 1954. Photo by Dr. Parry Bivens. Submitted by Zale Parry.

Ingredients

2 cucumbers, peeled and thinly sliced

Salt, pepper

1 cup sour cream

2-3 teaspoons vinegar

2-3 teaspoons sugar

Green chives, chopped (optional)

Instructions

Place cucumbers in a glass bowl. Salt well. Let stand 1/2 hour. Pour off all the liquid (squeeze lightly).

Add the sour cream, vinegar and sugar. Mix well. Taste. Add chives or not. Add pepper only. Chill. Serve with your catch.

*This tasty dish is simple to make and different from the vinegary cucumber salads so often served. It's as lovely and elegant as the lady herself.

Zale Parry on board *Moray*, Mart Toggweiler's boat, about 1959-1960. "See how happy I am to change ANOTHER roll of 12-exposure film? I still wore clothes under my dive suit! Style with fashion didn't matter. Comfort with no shivers did." Submitted by Zale Parry.

Zale Parry is an underwater pioneer, starting as a skin diver in 1947 and learning scuba in 1951. She worked early as an aquatic specialist, as an early underwater equipment tester, and as a hyperbaric science/research partner. In 1954, she set a woman's depth record of 209 feet. A *Sports Illustrated* cover girl in May, 1955, she became one of the country's first certified scuba instructors. In 1957, she became a film festival co-founder/co-producer, and, three years later, the first woman President of the Underwater Photographic Society.

Since 1954, she has been a SAG (Screen Actors' Guild) and AFTRA (American Federation of Television and Radio Artists) member, with credits including *Kingdom of the Sea,* the famous 1957-1961 *Sea Hunt* series (often playing the damsel in distress underwater), *GE Theatre, Wagon Train,* and more.

She received the Underwater Academy of Arts and Sciences' NOGI Distinguished Service Award in 1973, the Diving Equipment Marketing Association's (DEMA's) Reaching Out Award in 1993, the Women's Scuba Association, Scuba Diver of the Year Award in 1999, the Los Angeles County Parks and Recreation Education Award in 2001, and was inducted into the Women Divers Hall of Fame and the National Association of Underwater Instructors (NAUI) Hall of Fame in 2000. She was voted onto the NOGI Board of Directors in 2001.

With Albert Tillman, she co-authored *Scuba America, The Human History of Sport Diving in America,* which premiered in January 2001.

Zale Parry is known as someone who is ultimately involved, who made a difference, and who encouraged thousands of people, men as well as women, to experience the underwater world. She is the First Lady of American scuba diving.

Zale Parry with the book, *Dive America,* which she recently co-authored.

Bill Hamilton's
World Class Tomato Sandwich

"This recipe was designed to take advantage of fresh, vine-ripened tomatoes from my garden. It will work with other tomatoes, but they have to be very ripe. These sandwiches are as good as anything else I've ever eaten, and I want to share the method with anyone interested." -- Bill Hamilton

Ingredients

2 small, or 1 middle-sized, or 1/2 a large ripe tomato, peeled

2 slices good, firm bread; Arnold's Brick Oven is my choice. Pepperidge Farms is good, too

About 1/4 to 1/3 cup finely chopped heart of iceberg lettuce

Very thin slices of onion, 1 to 2 millimeter thick, from a 2-inch onion, or equivalent

Mayonnaise (Kraft's is preferred)

Grated cheddar cheese, about 1/4 cup

Salt

Pepper

Chips of your choice

Instructions

Making a good tomato sandwich takes time, so it is a good idea to have tortilla chips and salsa and Spanish or Greek black olives to nibble on during the process, and a drink or a beer. Another favorite is ripple potato chips.

Place 2 bread slices open upon a large dinner plate. Dip tomatoes into boiling water for 3 or 4 seconds to facilitate peeling, and peel; some prefer to peel tomatoes without the hot water, and if they are ripe enough, this can be quite easy. Slice into slices about 3/16 inch thick. Distribute slices evenly over one slice of bread, overlapping as necessary. There should be a full layer at least 3/16 to 1/4 inches thick; these slices go directly on the bread so some of the juice will be soaked up. Spread a generous layer (at least 1/16 inch) of mayo on the other slice of bread. Spread the finely chopped lettuce over the mayonnaise, covering evenly. Spread the 1/16-inch slices of onion over the lettuce, breaking apart the rings to cover loosely; too much onion will dominate the taste.

Moderately salt and heavily pepper both sides, on both the tomatoes and the lettuce and onions. Eat more chips and olives. Grate the cheese on the tomatoes, making an even layer about 1/4 inch thick, loosely packed. Don't forget the salt and pepper! Gently pack the cheese down with fingers or a spatula, then close that side of the sandwich onto the other. Or, use a spatula to assist in closing the lettuce side over the other. Stuff back in any cheese or lettuce that may fall out.

Carefully cut the sandwich in two, holding it down firmly at the same time. Don't cut the sandwich diagonally; the sharp corners are unsupported and the insides will tend to fall out. Use a fork or spatula when eating to replace any bits that fall out.

The best accompaniment is good potato chips, but tortilla chips or Fritos are good as well. Beer is a good drink, or white wine or soda.

BLT: Add a layer of very crisp, hot bacon, and you will get a BLT to die for.

This is a very scientifically designed sandwich (what else would you expect from Dr. Bill?), so just follow the instructions (after all, you follow his trimix tables, right?) and enjoy the best tomato sandwich.

Dr. R. W. Bill Hamilton is a physiologist and a former fighter pilot with 40 years of R&D experience in decompression of pressure, human performance, life support, and handling operational dive data. His laboratory work has involved commercial diving, deep saturation diving, HPNS, hyperbaric welding, chamber fire safety, oxygen tolerance, and spacecraft atmospheres. He has used his decompression program DCAP for a diverse set of projects, including producing the NOAA excursion and nitrox saturation tables, diving with neon, submarine escape methods, designing dive computers, and decompressing hyperbaric attendants.

His trimix tables were instrumental in the development of technical diving, and he has worked out practical methods of managing exposure to oxygen.

Although still a Texan, Bill Hamilton lives in Tarrytown, New York, on a hill overlooking the Hudson River and the Tappan Zee Bridge. He makes a practice of growing fine tomatoes in his garden every summer.

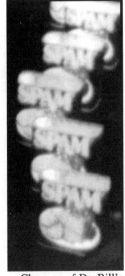

Close-up of Dr. Bill's famous Spam tie.

Brian Skerry's
Survival Grilled Cheese Sandwich

"Let me begin by stating that I am the last person on earth from whom to get a recipe. I am a strong proponent of making only reservations for dinner and when in remote regions without restaurants, I will eat anything available that requires nothing more than unwrapping.

"In August, 2002, I was working on a three-week assignment for *National Geographic Magazine* in a remote little town in Venezuela. Although there were a few restaurants nearby, I found very little that looked edible inside them. In one such establishment, I once ordered chicken and received a portion that was mostly uncooked. My Spanish was obviously not very good, as my request to send this dish back went unanswered.

"Three days after arriving in this village, I came down with a fever of 103-degrees. It seemed that I had ingested a parasite and was pretty sick. I landed flat on my back for three days. Fortunately, I had antibiotics with me and was able to get up and about on the 4th day. I was able to dive each morning, although I still felt lousy, and each afternoon, the fever would begin to rise again, making my nights quite miserable. During this whole time, I wasn't eating well, since the food there was terrible and probably unsafe. I also clearly had some form of dysentery, as nothing I ate stayed with me very long and I had frequent stomach pains.

"My assistant, Mark Conklin, and I were running out of ideas for meals and the little stores in town had limited supplies. One morning, as I lay on the couch in our room, the 13-year-old son of a scientist who was working with us began to prepare a grilled cheese sandwich. Mark and I had bought some cheese and bread in town, but it never occurred to us to make such fine delicacies.

"Amidst my fever-induced haze, I had a culinary epiphany! I watched as he buttered both sides of the bread, carefully placed the cheese in between, and placed the creation inside a frying pan on the gas stove. I was certain that even I could do this!

"That evening, after returning from a day at sea, I attempted the procedure myself. I am quite sure that Mark thought I was a genius as I served the sandwiches du fromage with a side of canned peas and a glass of Coke. We also found a couple of bags of pasta in an out-of-the-way shop, and the combination of grilled cheese sandwiches and pasta probably saved our lives during those three weeks.

"A couple of post scripts to the story: On the return home, I cleared customs in Miami and handed all of my luggage to an airline employee to re-check everything to my final destination. I asked her three times if everything was all set and she always said, 'Yes.' I never saw my gear again. $50,000 worth of photo equipment was all stolen. Four 70-lb. cases simply vanished with no explanation from the airline and no compensation, and the three weeks in Venezuela dehydrated me so much that I had a kidney stone attack which required hospitalization and ultrasound treatments." -- Brian Skerry

Ingredients

2 slices bread, 1 or 2 slices of cheese, butter or margarine

Instructions

Place 1 or 2 slices of cheese between two slices of bread (any type of bread will work).

Thinly butter the outsides of both slices of bread and place in a stovetop frying pan or almost any cooking surface. Grill until the cheese begins to melt and the bread turns brown.

If you are in a location where other food is available, you may enhance this recipe by adding such things as slices of ham, tomatoes, etc.

*This sandwich is a staple in most kitchens. I have fond memories of the ones my mother made, with the hot cheese oozing out. If you haven't made one for a while, try it again and experiment with different kinds of cheeses (e.g. cheddar or Swiss) and other additions as Brian suggests.

Brian Skerry is an assignment photographer for *National Geographic Magazine*, specializing in elusive underwater subjects. His images have also been featured in magazines such as *People, Sports Illustrated, US News and World Report, BBC Wildlife, GEO, Smithsonian, Esquire, Audubon, Outdoor Life, Wildlife Conservation, Yankee, Maxim, Men's Journal* and in countless publications worldwide.

He is the author/photographer of *Complete Wreck Diving* (with Henry Keatts; see page 58) and *A Whale On Her Own - the True Story of Wilma, The Beluga Whale,* and was the principal photographer for *Lost Subs*. His latest book, *Successful Underwater Photography* (with Howard Hall) was just released.

His assignments have taken him from shooting giant bluefin tuna in the Mediterranean to striped marlin off Baja, to sperm whales in the Azores. His work with shipwrecks and marine archaeology includes documenting historic sites such as the Civil War Ironclad *USS Monitor* and Confederate submarine *Hunley,* the pirate shipwreck *Whydah,* 8 German U-boats and the famed luxury liner, *Andrea Doria.* In his most recent work, he has lived on the ocean floor and photographed saturation divers/scientists inside the Aquarius Habitat, as well

Photo submitted by Brian Skerry.

as photographed seals beneath Canadian pack ice, hammerhead and tiger sharks in the Bahamas, Humboldt squid in the Sea of Cortez, and the D-Day shipwrecks off Normandy, France.

Gary Chesnut's
Savory Salmon Sandwich

"I have never found salmon to be better. Our family has enjoyed this little sandwich which came from my great grandmother and has been passed down." -- Gary Chesnut

Ingredients

12 Saltine crackers	1 egg
1 can of salmon	1 teaspoon of flour

Instructions

Takes the bones out of the salmon, crush the crackers, beat one egg and mix everything together with the flour. Make about four patties and fry in oil.

Season with salt and pepper to taste.

Makes a great sandwich, hot or cold.

This is a tasty, quick and easy sandwich. Thanks, Great-Grandma Chesnut!

Gary Chesnut has been diving since 1956, starting in the lakes of the Midwest and in Florida's Keys and caves. He became a PADI Instructor in 1968.

Since then, he has traveled extensively throughout the Caribbean, the Pacific and the Red Sea and has logged over 3,500 dives with camera in hand!

Photo submitted by Gary Chesnut

Gary was the first photographer to film the wreck of the *Lucius Newberry* in Lake Geneva and the schooner *Lumberman* in Lake Michigan, both of which had been missing for over 90 years.

His extensive diving has taken him to major shipwreck locations throughout the Great Lakes. He has won photographic awards in state, regional, national and international competitions. His work has been published in eight national magazines, calendars and books, and he has presented at major dive shows throughout the United States and Canada.

Gary recently retired as Excutive Director of the Kishwaukee Family YMCA in DeKalb, Illinois.

THIRD COURSE:
CATCH OF THE DAY

Our celebrity cooks obviously love seafood, especially if they've caught their dinner themselves. They also enjoy creating a party and sharing their fresh catch with their dive buddies:

ROBERT BALLARD's IFE New England Clam Bake .... page 46

BRET GILLIAM's Outdoor Steamed Lobster, Maine Style .... page 48

ELLSWORTH BOYD's Bahama Island Lobster Boats .... page 50

PETE NAWROCKY's Breakdown Smorgasbord .... page 52

JACK DRAFAHL's Bachelor Delight .... page 54

SUE DRAFAHL's Salmon & Loosen-Your-Weighbelt Sauce .... page 55

ERNEST BROOKS' Scallops a la "Just Love" .... page 56

HENRY KEATTS' Long Island Scalloped Scallops .... page 58

DAN CROWELL's Fried Smelt, Greek Style .... page 60

TEDDY TUCKER's Hashed Shark .... page 62

RICK ALLEN & CINDY BURNHAM's Shrimp and Grits .... page 64

DAN & BETTY ORR's DCS (Diver's Chili & Shrimp) .... page 66

WES SKILES' "Hey Now!" Special Sauce .... page 68

GLEN EGSTROM's Razzle-Dazzle Sizzling Fish .... page 70

DAN WAGNER's "FishyDan's" Delight .... page 72

DENNIS GAGNON's Barbecued Narc-ed Fish .... page 74

DAN LENIHAN's Old Baywatch Delight (camping version) .... page 76

MIKE & GEORGANN WACHTER's Perfect Perch/Abalone .... page 78

ROBERT MARX's "For Treasure and Pleasure" Sea Bass .... page 80

DICK BOYD's Campfire Whitefish .... page 82

Robert Ballard's
IFE New England Clam Bake

"I became active with the Boston Sea Rovers, one of the oldest diving clubs in the country, in the late 1960's when I moved to the East Coast from California. The love of the sea and of diving brought us together. So did a thirst for cold beer and lobsters steamed over a roaring campfire. After a fine day of good diving, we'd find a quiet bay on a deserted island, anchor, and swim ashore. We'd build a huge driftwood fire and steam the catch and a big sack of sweet corn in wet seaweed. We ate with our hands, ripping apart lobster shells and dunking our food in tin cans of melted butter. After a while, everybody was pretty greasy, so we'd just dive back into the water to wash off. I have many fond memories of those island feasts, which I described in my book, *Explorations*.

"This recipe is a variation of what we did in those days, with some suggestions and refinements thrown in from my crew at the Institute for Exploration." -- Robert Ballard

Prep Time: 3 hours 30 minutes   ***Cook Time:*** 1 hour 30 minutes   ***Ready In:*** 5 hours

Ingredients (Makes 20 servings)

20 small (1 pound) lobsters

20 pounds clams in shell, scrubbed

10 pounds mussels, cleaned and debearded

10 pounds cod

20 white potatoes

20 sweet potatoes

20 ears fresh corn

5 pounds bratwurst

5 pounds hot dogs

5 pounds pork sausage

3 pounds sweet onions

Instructions

At the beach, dig a hole in the sand with the approximate proportions: width = 2 feet, length = 4 feet, depth = 1 1/2 feet. Line the hole with stones from the beach. Build a fire inside the hole and cover with rocks from the beach. Heat the stones for 2 to 3 hours.

Remove coals and/or embers from the hole. Arrange hot stones evenly across the bottom of the hole. Place fresh 1/2 bushel seaweed (wet) on top of the stones.

Working quickly, layer the food on top of the seaweed. The food items should be layered evenly on top of each other in this order: clams, mussels, fish, sausage, hotdogs (wrapped in cheesecloth), onions, potatoes (white and sweet), corn, and finally lobsters.

Cover food with a clean, wet cloth. Place remaining seaweed on top of cloth.

Cover entire hole of food with a wet tarpaulin, sealing in the steam created by the hot stones and seaweed. Allow a very small amount of steam to escape to relieve pressure. Let the bake cook for 1 or more hours. The bake is completed when the potatoes are soft. Serve bake with lobster crackers and melted butter to dip the seafood in. Don't forget napkins -- you'll need'em!

*Napkins!??! You need to drape tarps around and cover yourself with a poncho because this is so luscious and so much fun, you will get messy!

Dr. Robert Ballard is founder and head of the Institute for Exploration (IFE) at Mystic Aquarium in Mystic, Connecticut. Specializing in deep-ocean archaeology, IFE's goal is to establish this new field of research utilizing evolving technology such as advanced mapping and imaging systems, underwater robotics and manned-submersibles. Another IFE objective is to share Dr. Ballard's most recent discoveries with millions of visitors to the Challenge of the Deep, part of a recent $52 million expansion at Mystic Aquarium.

Robert Ballard received his undergraduate degree in Geology and Chemistry from the University of California. He attended graduate school at the University of Southern California, the University of Hawaii's Graduate School of Oceanography and received his Ph.D. in Marine Geology and Geophysics from the University of Rhode Island.

Dr. Ballard is recognized as one of the premier spokesmen for marine research. For the past 20 years, he has participated in numerous educational programs, in particular, the National Geographic Society, including a two-year period when he hosted National Geographic's EXPLORER, shown on Turner Broadcasting.

Robert Ballard is most famous as the discoverer of several of the most historic shipwrecks on this planet, the first and most publicized of these being the ocean liner *R.M.S. Titanic* in 1985. Since then, he has located the remains of the German battleship *Bismarck*, 11 warships from the lost fleet of Guadalcanal, the U.S. aircraft carrier *Yorktown*, and, most recently, John F. Kennedy's *PT-109* from World War II.

After 30 years, Dr. Ballard retired from the Woods Hole Oceanographic Institution in 1997, where he was senior scientist and director of the Center for Marine Exploration. He is also founder of the JASON Project. JASON was established in 1989 after Robert Ballard received thousands of letters from school children wanting to know how he discovered the *R.M.S. Titanic*.

Dr. Robert Ballard on the bow of the Research Vessel *Connecticut.*

Bret Gilliam's
Outdoor Steamed Lobster, Maine Style

"For years, I made a point of visiting Maine whenever my schedule allowed. Living in the Caribbean induced a longing for a change of seasons as I was stuck in a perpetual 'endless summer' and the palm trees didn't change color in the fall. Maine has the sort of rugged coastal geography that always reminded me of the tropical islands, but with real trees and better seafood. So I would deliberately route my east-bound Atlantic crossings from Maine via the Azores and allow a week or two to cruise the coastal areas and islands during the spectacular summers. The sight of my 280-foot ship anchored in a quiet cove flying a Virgin Islands flag always attracted the attention of the local fishermen and we struck up long-standing friendships as I traded West Indian rum for their lobster, fresh from the ocean that morning.

"An old lobsterman, Elroy Johnson, from Bailey Island, taught me the proper way to cook lobster in the traditional 'shore bake' style. This method was simple, relatively fast, and tasted better than in the finest restaurants. It also lent itself to a fine afternoon appreciating the ocean view from the granite ledges adjacent the sandy beaches that rivaled the beauty of the South Pacific. Since this recipe was cooked entirely outside, no one was ever trapped in the galley slinging pots and pans, and there was little, if any, clean-up to bother with. Elroy also emphasized the importance of beer and wine consumption before, during and after the meal to better appreciate the food and the scenery. His counsel proved wise in all regards and I still cannot imagine a better way to eat lobster than on the beach in Maine with butter running down your arms and a pile of shell litter accumulating at your feet. The recipe works anywhere, thankfully... even in the Midwest." -- Bret Gilliam

Ingredients

This entire meal combines the key ingredients of the classic Maine lobster bake: clams, fresh corn, and Maine lobster. You'll need a cauldron of some type. Typically, an old horse trough was the preferred vessel for large parties, but I found that a standard 15-gallon metal wash tub, available at any hardware store, is perfect for up to about 10 persons. You'll also need some rock seaweed, kelp, or similar marine seaweed, some dry firewood and 3 bottles of beer, and you're ready to go.

Instructions

Contain and control your beach fire. I recommend laying your fire site in the mid-tidal zone where the rising tide will extinguish it completely and also take away your waste. Start your fire and let it get roaring a bit and begin to settle down before positioning the wash tub about a foot over the flames. Pour about four inches of sea water in the bottom of the wash tub and pour three 12-ounce beers in as well for flavor.

As soon as the water boils, add 2 lobsters per person to the bottom of the tub and cover with a layer of seaweed about 4 inches thick. Spread an even layer of fresh corn still in the husk on top of the seaweed and cover with another layer of seaweed. Now add approximately a half pound of fresh clams (steamers) per person on that layer of seaweed and cover with a final layer of seaweed.

Let the whole thing cook approximately 20 minutes. You can be sure that it's done if you peel back the top layer of seaweed and the clams have opened. This ensures that the lobster, corn and clams will be perfectly cooked. You'll see the steam rising from the seaweed and thrill to the intoxicating aroma. Remove the seaweed and discard.

The clams and lobster can be served on plates or newspaper. Husk the corn and serve together with the seafood. You'll want plenty of melted butter for dipping. A little lime or lemon squeezed into the butter is a nice touch. Best enjoyed with ice-cold beer or white wine. Plenty of it! Since the waste is all organic, it can go out with the tide.

Be careful to use heavy gloves when removing the food. It will be extremely hot and can burn unprotected skin. Let the food cool in the air naturally while eating the clams first. By the time they're finished, the lobster will have cooled sufficiently to eat with your hands.

You NEED to get messy and eat this with your hands. If your shirt doesn't have to go to the laundry afterwards, you weren't doing it right.

This is not just a great meal, it's a great experience. Go for it!

Bret Gilliam began diving in 1958 and has since logged over 15,000 dives, including holding the world record for deep diving on conventional scuba (475 feet in 1993). Considered a pioneer in the earliest development of technical diving programs, he founded TDI in 1994 and that training agency has grown to be the largest tech certification program in the world. He has been professionally full time in the diving industry since 1971 after serving in the U.S. Navy as a diver working on film projects filming submarines. Since then, he has carved an enviable success story with his investments in liveaboard vessels, resort operation, training agencies, manufacturing and publishing.

He is a licensed USCG Merchant Marine Master and has captained vessels up to 525' long through the world's oceans. He is the ex-President and CEO of UWATEC, ex-Chairman of NAUI, and was one of the principals in Ocean Quest International, the largest diving operation in the world. author of over 500 articles and 17 books, he is noted for his technical expertise and trademark sense of humor.

Currently Bret is Publisher of *Fathoms Magazine*, Chairman of Ocean Tech, and President and CEO of TDI and SDI. He is 52 years old and lives on a semi-private island in Maine after spending over 20 years in the Caribbean. A self-made millionaire, he is determined to never have a job that requires him to wear long pants, a tie, or real shoes.

Photo submitted by Bret Gilliam.

Ellsworth Boyd's
Bahama Island Lobster Boat

"How in the world could a shipwreck lead to my favorite recipe? Strange as it sounds, that's what happened to my dive buddy, Jim Kelly and I years ago when we were exploring a shipwreck off Freeport, Grand Bahama Island.

"While searching for clues to the ship's identity, we came upon a half a dozen spiny lobsters hiding beneath the boiler. Since lobsters were in season and we were on a meager budget, we knew exactly where our next dinner was coming from.

"A friendly old Bahamian dockmaster, spotting our prizes when we returned to shore, offered us 'the greatest lobster recipe in the Bahamas' in exchange for a bottle of rum. We obliged him, joking on the way back to our quarters that we had probably been 'taken for a perfectly good bottle of rum.'

"Nothing could have been further from the truth. It turned out to be the best lobster dish we had ever savored, and one that we still indulge in and share with friends and relatives." -- Ellsworth Boyd.

Ingredients

1 medium-to-large lobster tail per serving, free
from shell & cut into bite-sized chunks

Aluminum foil

1/4 lb. of butter

1 bottle of light rum

1 can of Dole's chunk pineapple

An oven broiler or grill

Instructions

Slit the lobster tail vertically down the underside with a sharp knife. Then turn the tail over and use the heel of your hand to press down on the shell until it cracks. Use both hands to break apart the tail, as if you were breaking open the shell of a peanut. Separate the meat form the shell and cut it into bite-sized chunks.

Take several layers of aluminum foil and shape a little boat for the lobster meat. Spread the meat out; don't stack the chunks one on top of the other. Make sure the boat's gunnels are at least three to four inches higher than the meat. Also be sure there are no leaks in your boat or you will lose some of its main ingredients.

Pour one ounce of light rum over the cargo. Then pour one ounce of the same rum into a glass, along with your favorite mixer and sip this while you load the boats. Don't drink too much too soon, or both you and the boats will be loaded! Pour 2 ounces of the syrup from the canned pineapple over the cargo. Load each boat with the pineapple chunks, letting some of the lobster meat show through. Put a thin sliver of butter in the bow and stern of each boat. Then, using the oven, place on a pan and broil the boats for about 12 to 15 minutes. Follow a similar procedure for charcoal, placing the boats over hot coals for the same amount of time.

NOTE: Build as many boats as you need. If there are a lot of guests, you might launch a whole fleet. Teach everbody the words to the song, "Shrimp boats" ("Shrimp boats are coming, there's dancing tonight, shrimp boats are coming, their sails are in sight! Why don't you hurry, hurry, hurry home, why don't you hurry, hurry, hurry home. Shrimp boats are coming, their sails are in sight!" But be sure and substitute "lobster" for "shrimp." "Lobster boats are coming, their sails are in sight, etc." Have a drink when you launch the boats and another one to welcome them home!

Propose a toast to the wise old Bahamian who shared this tantalizing treat in exchange for a meager bottle of rum.

Ellsworth Boyd, a native Marylander, learned to dive when he was a lifeguard in Ft. Lauderdale, Florida. Although his initial interest was spearfishing, he soon traded his speargun for an underwater camera.

He became hooked on shipwrecks and ship research after photographing and exploring historical vessels sunk off Florida and the Bahamas. His research on wrecks and other diving topics led to hundreds of articles that have appeared throughout the years in major dive publications in the United States, Canada, England, Italy and Germany.

Ellsworth Boyd brings up a spiny lobster for a special Bahamian Lobster Boat recipe. Photo by Bob Allen. Submitted by Ellsworth Boyd.

Ellsworth's "Wreck Facts" column in *Skin Diver Magazine* was widely read throughout the world. He is also Professor Emeritus, College of Education, Towson University, Towson, Maryland. Ellsworth and his family reside in White Hall, Maryland.

Pete Nawrocky's
Breakdown Smorgasbord

"As with many people, the love of diving has often eaten up more money than it should. Driving a beat-up van with a cantankerous motor has led to more than one stranding at a beach.

"Our van broke down after the dive and we had two catch bags full of flounder and crabs. No ice was available and the nearest bait station was closed on a late Sunday evening.

"We had planned on moving to another place but had to make do with what was in the truck. Jackie (now my wife) and I had grabbed a few last-minute things for the trip, including the onions and half a bag of hot dog rolls. The plan was to purchase what we needed on the road. Cooking utensils were not a problem and there was a case of Molson Ale in the back. Just before we left, I had tossed the Coleman stove into the truck. Since we had nowhere to go, we just rummaged through the van and made do.

"The beer got into the recipe when Jackie was concerned about the onions burning in the pan. I just walked over and poured the rest of the ale I was drinking into the skillet. This went on to steaming the crabs and clams in beer.

"We got the truck started the next morning after I gapped the 'points' with a zip tab I found on the beach. If THAT doesn't date the story, you're too young to know." -- Pete Nawrocky

Ingredients

Fresh flounder (preferably the ones you caught)

Any type of edible shellfish or crabs

2 large Vidalia onions

Your choice of beer or ale

Bread of your choice or hot dog rolls

Instructions

Fillet the flounder, wash off the crabs and shellfish.

Chop the onions up and place in a large skillet. Add approximately 1 to 1 1/2 cups of beer. Spread the onions out so that they are thicker than the beer layer.

Cover and heat over a medium flame. When the beer begins to boil, place the flounder fillets on top of the onions. Be careful not to allow the fillets to fall into the fluid. The fillets will now steam over the bed of onions.

Turn the fillets as they reach proper texture and are cooked thoroughly.

After cooking, place the fillets on hot dog buns and garnish with the onions or condiments of your choice.

While enjoying the fillets, place the remainder of the onions and cooked beer into a large pot. After bringing the mixture to a boil, add the crabs and shellfish and cook thoroughly: usually 5 minutes per pound. Do not undercook shellfish.

The beer adds a nutty flavor while the sweet Vidalia onions add a distinctive sweetness.

*There's nothing more fun than cooking out on the beach after a day of diving. This recipe proves that even "making do" can be delicious!

Pete Nawrocky has over 25 years of diving and underwater photography experience. He specializes in diverse environments and marine life found in the Northeast. Pete's work has been published in most scuba diving periodicals such as Skin Diver, Immersed, NAUI Sources and Dive Journal, as well as in books and international publications.

He has received both the Beneath The Sea Diver of the Year Award and a NAUI Outstanding Service Award. His work is on permanent display in the Intrepid Air, Sea and Space Museum in New York City.

Jack Drafahl's
Bachelor Delight

"In my bachelor days, this dish was one of my favorite personal creations. It's surprisingly good and simple to make. I still like to make it when my wife, Sue, goes out of town. Our daughter dreads her mother's trips because she knows I will make this recipe and she hates it. I don't know why. I think it's great." -- Jack Drafahl

Ingredients

1 can cream of mushroom soup

1 can tuna, drained

1 can corn, drained

English muffins, split

Instructions

Pour ingredients from cans into saucepan. Heat gently. When hot, pour over toasted English muffins.

Jack, your daughter's too hard on you. Thank goodness Jack is married now and can eat Sue's wonderful salmon [see next page].

Jack and Sue Drafahl are a husband-and-wife team of professional undersea photojournalists, lecturers and multimedia producers. Their articles appear in noted periodicals like *Sport Diver, Skin Diver, Petersen's Photographic, Rangefinder* and many more. They are Platinum Pro 5000 Divers with over 30 years of diving experience and enjoy teaching seminars worldwide on all aspects of photography, both topside and underwater. They were named Beneath The Sea Divers of the Year in 1996. Sue was an inaugural member of the Women Divers Hall of Fame and now serves as a Trustee. She has produced DEMA's Reaching Out Awards Program for 10 years and has participated in film festivals from coast to coast.

They have been involved in the digital transition since the early 1980's and are software and hardware Beta testers for companies like Adobe, Applied Science Fiction, Corel and Ulead Systems. They have written two books, *Digital Imaging for the Underwater Photographer* and *Photo Salvage with Adobe Photoshop*. Three additional books, *Advanced Digital Camera Techniques* and *Step-By-Step Basic Digital - A Guide for Beginning Photographers* will be released in Spring, 2003 and *A Complete Guide to Photoshop-Compatible Plug-in Filters,* which will be available Spring, 2004.

Sue Drafahl's
Salmon and Loosen-Your-Weightbelt Sauce

"I stole this recipe from my sister. Since we [Jack and I] now live on the Oregon coast, fresh salmon is often available." -- Sue Drafahl.

Ingredients

Use fresh salmon filets rather than salmon steaks. Allow about 1/2 pound of fish per person

Sauce: 1 stick butter

1 tablespoon Dijon mustard

1 tablespoon ketchup

1 tablespoon teriyaki sauce

1 tablespoon white wine

Instructions

Melt the butter and blend all the sauce ingredients on low heat -- do not boil.

Divide the sauce and baste with half and reserve half as a dip. Put the salmon on the barbecue and baste with sauce several times as it is cooking. Once the salmon flakes easily when tested with a fork, remove it from the barbecue.

Serve with wild rice and green beans sautéed with sesame oil and covered with slivered almonds. The remaining sauce can be used as a dip.

This is best enjoyed with good friends and a chilled Chardonnay wine from the Oregon vineyards.

The salmon and sauce combination is absolutely luscious and its delicate pink is beautifully complemented by the green beans.

Photo submitted by Jack & Sue Drafahl.

Ernest Brooks'
Scallops a la "Just Love"

Photo submitted by Ernie Brooks.

"On board my Alaskan trawler, "Just Love," I prepare this as only a sampler for my students who then take over the cooking duties for all of our offshore expeditions -- preparing pastas and their family specialties for the crew." -- Ernie Brooks

Ingredients

10 large rock scallops freshly picked from the California Channel Islands (limit = 10)

2 buds garlic -- fresh, not packaged, chopped

Butter -- 1/2 pound salted

Dash salt (sea)

2 pinches pepper (black)

1/3 cup olive oil

Instructions

Begin by slicing scallops to 1/4 inch steaks. Use only the mussel portion. Wash in sea water. Use 10-inch iron skillet.

Pour in olive oil and bring to high heat. Add butter and garlic.

Add scallops when butter is at the boiling point. Scallops should cover skillet in a single layer.

After 1 minute, turn with fork. Add salt and pepper.

After 1 minute, serve from the skillet.

This is <u>so</u> easy and <u>so</u> luscious! But if I were one of his students, I would find this dish to be a hard act to follow.

Ernest Brooks II, Ambassador to the Marine Environment, Photographer, Adventurer, Diver and Educator, was born to be a photographer. His Portuguese ancestry, rich in men-of-the-sea, virtually insured the ocean environment would play an important role in his life. As the son of Ernest H. Brooks, founder of the internationally-renowned Brooks Institute of Photography, Ernest Brooks was destined to follow in his father's footsteps for part of his life's journey before forging his own path.

He graduated from Brooks Institute, served on the school's executive staff and in 1971 assumed the office of the President, a position he held until 2000 when the institute was sold to Career Education Corporation (CEC).

As a noted professional photographer, educator and ambassador to the industry, Ernest Brooks has won international acclaim for underwater photography and audio/visual presentations. As a working professional, he also contributed to numerous magazines and organizations, including The Cousteau Society, *California Highways, Ocean Realm,* Monterey Bay Aquarium and *Natural Wildlife.*

He is the recipient of many honors and awards, including the 1973 "Triton Award" Inner Space Pacifica, Hawaii, the 1975 NOGI Award from The Underwater Society of America, the 1977 "National Award" from the Professional

Signing prints of his underwater images, Oct., 2002.

Photographers of America, and, most recently, the 1996 "Partner's Award" from the American Oceans Campaign for his lifelong commitment and dedication to our oceans.

Ernest Brooks has been a trailblazer in the development of underwater photographic equipment and technique. And though he has harnessed and implemented much of that new technology, at a time when a plethora of color underwater photographs illustrate magazines and glossy brochures, he favors black-and-white. His dramatic marine images are displayed in his book, *Silver Seas, A Photographic Retrospective.*

Henry Keatts'
Long Island Scalloped Scallops

Photo submitted by Henry Keatts.

"In 1972, my first semester at Suffolk Community College (Long Island, New York), one of my biology students invited me to join him on a scallop dive. During that dive, we gathered about two bushels of Long Island bay scallops. After the dive, we had the arduous task of shucking the mollusks. In the U.S., we eat only the adductor muscle that closes the valves. Scallops are bivalves and have two parts (valves) to the shell.

"Having moved to Long Island from Texas, Carole (my wife) and I had experienced scallops only in restaurants. Now Carole was faced with the task of finding a recipe. After trying several mediocre recipes, we found our favorite in *A Treasury of Great Recipes* by Mary and Vincent Price. The opening statement in this treasury of recipes reads: 'To many hands in many lands. Our home is the achievement of many hands laboring with love to make it beautiful. Our table reflects the many lands we have traveled in and the hands that fed us. We thank them all for enriching our lives in so many ways and hope that through the pages of this book, we may enrich yours as well.'

"Carole found a recipe for scallops in the section on French restaurants. The Hotel de la Poste is in the medieval town of Beaune, France, surrounded by the vineyards of Burgundy. The hotel is on the Street of the Cask-Makers; after all, wine is the chief industry of this quaint town. The restaurant Chevillot A Beaune is located in the hotel. The owner-chef gave the following recipe to the Prices for publication in their cookbook. They called the recipe 'Coquilles St. Jacques Baumaniere.'

"For the next decade, during scallop season, I gathered bushels of scallops and Carole would frequently prepare Coquilles St. Jacques Baumaniere using fresh or frozen scallops. Unfortunately, by the early '80's, a brown tide (microscopic marine organisms) had decimated the scallop population which has not recovered." -- Henry "Hank" Keatts

Ingredients

1 1/2 pounds scallops

1 tablespoon shallots, chopped

Salt and white pepper

1/2 cup dry vermouth

1 cup cream

1 tablespoon flour

4 tablespoons softened butter

Instructions

Wash scallops, put in saucepan with: shallots, salt, pepper and dry vermouth.

Bring liquid to a boil, cover pan, simmer over low heat for 2 minutes only.

Remove scallops with slotted spoon and divide into 4 scallop shells.

Sauce: Add cream, boil rapidly until cream is reduced and sauce has syrup consistency.

Combine flour and butter. Reduce heat and gradually stir in butter, bit by bit.

Pour sauce over scallops and heat in hot oven for 5 minutes.

*This dish has a wonderful flavor. If you don't have scallop shells (and let's face it, some of us have to go "fishing" at the grocery store), use ramekins, a muffin tin or whatever you have.

Henry Keatts is Professor of Biology and Oceanography, Suffolk Community College, Long Island, New York. In addition to being widely published in his field, Henry is the author of *New England's Legacy of Shipwrecks* and *Field Guide to Sunken U-boats, Guide to Shipwreck Diving: New York and New Jersey,* and *Beachcomber's Guide: From Cape Cod to Cape Hatteras*. He is co-author of the *Dive into History* series *(Vol. 1: Warships, Vol. 2: U.S. Submarines,* and *Vol. 3: U-boats)*, and, with Brian Skerry [see page 42], *Complete Wreck Diving: A Guide to Diving Wrecks*. Also, he is co-author of *The Bell Tolls: Shipwrecks and Lighthouses* series *(Vol. 1: Block Island* and *Vol. 2: Eastern Long Island)*. He is a Fellow of the prestigious Explorers Club (Manhattan, New York), and associate member of the Boston Sea Rovers, and an honorary member of the Gillmen Club Hartford, CT) and the Adirondack Underwater Explorers (Saratoga Springs, NY). His underwater photography complements both his academic and avocational pursuits.

Over the past 22 years, he has presented 194 slide/lecture presentations on marine biology and maritime history to such varied groups as the U.S. Naval War College, service organizations (Kiwanis, Lions and Rotary), historical societies, Museum of Natural History, Explorers Club, New York Aquarium at Coney Island, dive clubs, libraries, church groups, and colleges and universities (U.S. Merchant Marine Academy, Harvard, Temple, Brown, and George Washington, to name a notable few).

He has presented programs at underwater festivals in the following U.S. cities: Boston, New York, Philadelphia, Washington, Atlanta, Miami, Houston, Chicago and San Diego.

Hank & Carole Keatts at a recent Boston Sea Rovers Show.

Dan Crowell's
Fried Smelt, Greek Style

"While in Greece on the 1998 expedition to dive the *Britannic,* we arrived in the port of Piraeus at about 4:30 AM local time. Dutifully we stacked our luggage in a neat row awaiting the opening of the ticket booth to purchase a ticket for the ferry which would take us on the last leg to our final destination, Kea, the island that would be our base for the expedition. Of course, when the booth finally opened, we soon found that we had stacked all of our crap in the wrong place and in the way of just about everything as the morning bustle began to stir.

"After what felt like a month of travel, we arrived at around 9 AM on Kea. Hungry, we investigated the local eateries for a meal of anything that didn't have to be unwrapped, going from one establishment to the next trying to find someone to serve us, but many were closed. We finally found a man outside his shop who, in very broken English, said, 'Sit, sit.' We all accepted his invitation. He passed out what appeared to be the only three or four menus he had, which really didn't do us much good, as none of us spoke Greek. Looking at the illustrations on the building, we all pointed to the one thing we recognized - grilled cheese. The man acknowledged our request by answering, 'OOOh! Two toast!' which we soon found out was much more correct than grilled cheese. What the man finally brought out was exactly that - two pieces of toasted bread with a slice of cheese in between. Two toasts!

" After several days of this type of quandary (for example, one restaurant would be open at noon one day, and not until 5 PM the next day, and not at all on another day), we realized that many of the shops and restaurants at that port were open only in accordance with the port's scheduled arrivals of the larger ferries which would dock there for several hours on a varying daily schedule.

"Near the final days of the expedition, Kostas (the owner of the Greek Dive Center) took a few of us on a short ride to a smaller harbor just over the hill, where he bought us lunch. It was a nice little restaurant that was open every day at the same time right next to several others jammed into a quaint cove overlooking the harbor. They served these fried little fish like French fries with eyes and fins. These will definitely wow your guests at any occasion, from a Sunday football gathering to a gourmet delight." -- Dan Crowell

The trick here is to actually find the smelt. Go to your local fish market and ask for a few pounds of baby smelt, in the 2-to-3-inch range. If that fails, try the bait shop.

Ingredients

2 eggs

1/4 cup of milk

1 cup flour

1/2 teaspoon salt

1/2 teaspoon pepper

Instructions

In a medium size mixing bowl, beat eggs and milk together.

In another bowl, add flour, salt and pepper.

Adding a handful at a time, put the smelt into the egg mix, coating them thoroughly.

Remove from egg mix and put into the flour mix, again coating them thoroughly.

Drop into deep fryer or pan fry until golden brown.

Add garnish and serve with traditional Greek Tzaziki sauce.

Serving "French fries" with eyes and fins sure sounds like divers' party food to me!

Dan Crowell is a professional diver and skipper of one of the most famous dive boats in the world, *Seeker*. He is a certified commercial diver, SDI/TDI Instructor trainer, former Vice Chairman of the Philadelphia chapter of the Explorers Club, a member of the Rutgers University Institute of Marine and Coastal Science Research dive team, and the President of his own company, Deep Explorers, Inc., a commercial dive service and recreational diver training facility.

Dan is one of the pioneers of technical diving and created the protocol for technical wreck diving in the Northeast, leading the way to deep wreck exploration and discovery of many unknown shipwrecks in the Northeast off the coasts of New York and New Jersey. Dan has led more expeditions to the ill-fated ocean liner, *Andrea Doria,* than anyone in the world.

In recent years, Dan has set his sights on filmmaking and has become one of the area's most notable underwater videographers. His footage has been used by all of the major networks, as well as many cable TV shows and in several documentaries.

Teddy Tucker's
Hashed Shark

"Hashed shark is a favorite dish of mine. It is delicious and extremely nutritious and worth the effort. It is important to use a small 'puppy' shark caught when the moon is bright because only then is the shark's liver good (it's cream-colored instead of gray).

"I cook and enjoy my cooking. I hope you do, too." -- Teddy Tucker

Ingredients

1 small Dusky Shark, 6 to 8 lbs., caught when
     the moon is bright (see above)

Red hot peppers (blended or chopped)

Thyme

Parsley

Sweet bell peppers

Instructions

Cut livers into small pieces, and place in heavy pan over very low fire until livers are melted (95% of livers is oil). Livers smell bad but taste goooooood.

Now empty contents of shark's stomach, remove fins and tail and discard.

Cut shark body into 4 or 5 pieces. Put into large pot of boiling water.

When cooked, remove from water and remove skin and cartilage.

Squeeze all water from shark, using cheesecloth or hands.

Put squeezed shark back into clean pot.

Toss with wooden spoon until dry, adding red hot peppers, lots of thyme, lots of parsley, blended sweet bell peppers.

Toss more, make well, and add some hot oil to crumbled shark.

Toss, dry, add more oil until dry, toss, toss, until all oil is used.

Toss until shark has absorbed all oil from livers.

Serve in bowls.

MAKE YOUR OWN HOT SAUCE: Blend Scotch Bonnet Peppers, and/or Bird Peppers, seeds too, in rum. Bottle and cork the sauce. Let stand a week or longer. Throw blender away. Great served in fish chowder!

*This dish alone would be worth the trip to Bermuda!

Teddy Tucker in Bermuda. Photo courtesy of Ellsworth Boyd.

Teddy Tucker, legendary treasure hunter and ocean explorer, is Bermuda's own treasure. A native Bermudan, he learned to dive as a teenager in 1938 while working at an aquarium on the North Shore where he pumped air down to tourists who were trying out hardhat equipment. On slow days, he tried it out himself. At the age of 16, Teddy worked as a sailor on board a four-masted schooner out of Maine, and in 1942, he enlisted in the British Royal Navy, seeing action in the Pacific during World War II. He tested dive gear and learned about underwater salvage.

After the war, Teddy launched a salvage business back in Bermuda, where he made a living locating scrap copper and brass underwater. In 1955, his exploration of the 1595 Spanish wreck of the *San Pedro,* which turned out to be one of Bermuda's richest treasure finds, yielded an ornate gold cross with 7 huge emeralds in it. Teddy's reputation was made! Since then, he has salvaged considerable gold and silver from dozens of Bermuda's oldest shipwrecks. He was awarded the Member of British Excellence by Queen Elizabeth II in 1994, and in 1998, Teddy helped establish the Professional Shipwreck Explorers Association. His work continues today with deep sea exploration.

Rick Allen & Cindy Burnham's
Shrimp and Grits

"My girlfriends and I [Cindy] were planning an all-girls annual get-together in Beaufort, South Carolina. It was about the same time as the movie *Forest Gump* was showing. We had seen the film and loved the scene where Forrest and Bubba are scrubbing the floor, and Bubba talks on and on about all the ways shrimp can be cooked. So we decided to have a Bubba Shrimp Weekend. We would have shrimp for breakfast, lunch and dinner. In the course of that weekend, my friend, Lolita, turned us on to the great Southern tradition of Shrimp and Grits. Now it's a favorite of Rick's, too!" -- Cindy Burnham

Ingredients (for 6 people)

1 1/2 to 2 pounds fresh shrimp, peeled and deveined

1 cup grits

1 cup sharp cheddar cheese

4 cups water

2 cups milk or cream

1/2 cup margarine or butter

1 tablespoon finely chopped fresh parsley

salt to taste

Instructions

Slowly stir grits and salt into briskly boiling water. Reduce heat to medium-low. Cover and cook for 7 to 10 minutes or until thickened, stirring occasionally.

Then slowly add the milk or cream. Cook on low heat for 20 minutes. Grits will become creamier if you cook uncovered.

Add the cheese - stir it in.

Now it's time to sauté the shrimp in the butter and parsley. Be very careful not to overcook the shrimp! Shrimp should be very light in color.

Stir the shrimp and butter into the grits!

Tip: For thinner, soupy grits, add more milk.

This dish is versatile enough to be breakfast, brunch, lunch or supper - it tastes good any time of the day! Even Northerners who think they don't like grits will like this.

Rick Allen is an award-winning broadcast video producer and videographer who has been diving the oceans of the world and shooting video since 1983. Co-founder of Nautilus Productions in 1997, his work has appeared on A&E, ABC, CBS, Discovery, The Learning Channel, 48 Hours, ESPN, Fox Sports and more. Rick has followed SWAT teams on drug busts, landed on the aircraft carrier *USS America,* weathered broadcasts during hurricanes, traveled from Cuba to Kazakstan with the 82nd Airborne, and worked side-by-side with 9-foot Sand Tiger Sharks during underwater expeditions. Rick is focused on documentary productions and providing freelance videography and underwater video to broadcast clients, and he has presented his underwater videos at all of the major scuba shows. He is an avid wreck diver and shark lover who can be found most weekends diving the Graveyard of the Atlantic off North Carolina.

Photo submitted by Rick Allen and Cindy Burnham.

Cindy Burnham's 20 years of photojournalism reflects the extremes of humanity and nature. From the intensity of the warfare reflected on an American soldier's face, to the

surrealness of an underwater morgue of an Atlantic shipwreck, her images have appeared on the covers and pages of *Newsweek, New York Times,* and the Time-Life book, *Sky Soldiers.* Additional publications include *Army Times, USA Today, Philadelphia Inquirer,* and numerous other monthly, weekly, and daily periodicals. She is co-founder of Nautilus Productions, a freelance photography and video company, as well as the assignment editor and senior photographer at the *Fayetteville Observer.* Her work has repeatedly been recognized by both North and South Carolina's press photography associations.

Dan & Betty Orr's
DCS (Diver's Chili with Shrimp)

"This recipe is the result of ongoing 'Chili Cook-Off' competitions at various places we've worked. We finally said, 'We can't be outdone. Let's come up with something different!' And we did!" -- Dan and Betty Orr

Ingredients

1 can (30 oz.) light red kidney beans

1 can (16 oz.) chili hot beans

1 can (15 oz.) chunky tomato sauce with celery and green bell peppers

1/2 cup Thick 'n Chunky salsa (Note: We use MILD, but suit your taste buds and gastro-intestinal tract)

1/2 cup chopped onions

1/3 lb. peeled and deveined fresh shrimp OR 1 can (6.5 oz.) tiny shrimp

1 tablespoon + 1 teaspoon chili powder

Instructions

In a large pot, mix all beans, tomato sauce, 1/4 cup salsa, onions, and 1 tablespoon chili powder.

Simmer for 1 hour, stirring often.

Dump fresh shrimp (or drained tiny shrimp) into ziploc bag with reserved 1/4 cup of salsa and 1 teaspoon chili powder.

Seal ziploc bag and encourage shrimp to get acquainted for 1 hour.

A few minutes before serving, dump shrimp mixture into pot of simmering chili ingredients and stir well (NOTE: DO NOT OVERCOOK SHRIMP unless you have a fondness for rubber!)

Additional comments: Serves 6 hungry people or 2 divers.

Those consuming this chili are advised to sleep in a well-ventilated area and at a safe distance from open flames. NOTE: Originators of this recipe cannot be held responsible for possible incendiary results if open flames are not extinguished, or for the potential social repercussions of respiratory embarrassment.

*This chili is absolutely delicious and a nice variation from chilis using meat. It isn't too spicy, but you won't feel like a cowardly pantywaist either.

Dan Orr is Vice President and Chief Operating Office at Divers Alert Network (DAN), responsible for all of the day-to-day running of the organization. He started at DAN in 1991 and developed the internationally successful DAN Oxygen First Aid Course. Prior to DAN, he was the Associate Diving Officer at Florida State University. Dan has spoken at many national and international sumposia and has authored and contributed to many books and magazine articles. He has been the recipient of many awards, including the Leonard

Greenstone Award for Diving Safety in 1995, the prestigious NOGI Award from the Academy of Underwater Arts & Sciences in 1996, and the "Our World - Underwater" Award in 1997.

Betty Orr was scuba certified in 1975 while attending graduate school at Wright State University. She is Director of Insurance Services for Divers Alert Network (DAN) Services, and she has developed and introduced training programs, edited and co-authored periodicals, training manuals and textbooks, lectured at the most prestigious diving conventions on topics regarding diving fitness, subjects specific to women in diving, and conducted workshops on dive accident statistics, dive safety, oxygen first aid and the diving environment. She is an inaugural member of the Women Divers Hall of Fame.

Photo submitted by Dan & Betty Orr.

Wes Skiles'
"Hey Now!" Special Sauce

"This is a homemade sauce that I created and perfected over the years. I started out trying to make tartar sauce but had no idea what to truly do. As people started to exclaim how good it was with my grilled grouper, I continued to perfect the mixture.

"Wes' 'Hey Now' Special Sauce can be used several ways with popular results:

1.) As a glaze before and during grilling,

2.) As a side complement for dipping individual bites,

3.) As a spread on Wes' grouper sandwiches,

4.) As a 'to die for' substitution for tartar sauce with fried grouper (oh my....)

"This is a fun, easy to make sauce that will get oooh's and aaah's from your guest.

"I love to spoon it on lightly over fresh grilled fish, but it's really hard to beat with fresh fried grouper.

"Make sure you use lots of really fresh garlic and fresh dill when you can find it.

"Zatarain's is an excellent cajun spice blend that gives Wes' 'Hey Now' Special Sauce a nice pop. Try it. You'll like it!" -- Wes Skiles

Ingredients

Mayonnaise	Dill weed
Mustard	Lemon
Garlic	Zatarain's Cajun Spice Blend
Cream of tartar	Olive oil

Instructions

Mix even parts of mayo and mustard -- 1 tablespoon of each.

Add one teaspoon of olive oil, dice a clove of fresh garlic, add fresh squeezed lemon and dill weed (from bottle okay).

Add cream of tartar to increase base consistency.

Add Zatarain's cajun spice to personal taste.

A nice "pop" is right -- this deliciously fresh and sassy sauce leaves you laughing and saying "Hey now!"

I asked Wes for his "Biosketch" and he sent me this sketch of a bionic diver -- a self-portrait.

Wes Skiles is best known in the diving industry for his work in motion pictures and still photography. He has made over 5,000 dives in the last 27 years, including the Enchanted River project, the world's longest underground river, a record 320-foot mixed gas dive in the Wakulla Springs, rappelling over a kilometer into the earth for National Geographic in system Huaultia in Southern Mexico, and being among the first to successfully film sperm whales, the largest toothed whale on the planet.

His work has appeared on major television networks worldwide. He has produced films with titles such as "African Shark Safari," about face-to-face encounters with Great White sharks, "Most Dangerous Science," a cave diving exploration science adventure, and the IMAX film "Journey Into Amazing Caves" featuring fantastic images of the underwater cave world of the Yucatan.

Wes is currently using the state-of-the-art High Definition format and is pioneering its use in extreme environments such as the "Ice Island Project," an expedition to Antarctica to study and film the B-15 Iceberg.

Wes' enthusiasm and unique wit make him one of the most admired and sought-after presenters on the show circuit today.

Glen Egstrom's
Razzle-Dazzle Sizzling Fish

"I got this wonderful recipe from a friend in Santa Barbara who taught cooking for many years. Once, when I was demonstrating this dish in front of a cooking class, I was in a hurry and, by mistake, poured the oil on top of the soy sauce in a hot pan. It exploded! A fine mist of soy and oil sprayed all over everything, including me and the ceiling! We were able to clean everything except, of course, the ceiling. The lesson to be learned is don't cover hot liquid with oil! So read and follow this recipe carefully - AND TAKE YOUR TIME!" -- Glen Egstrom

Ingredients

1 pound halibut, orange roughy, or other mild white fish

1/2 cup soy sauce

1 teaspoon sesame oil

1 or 2 green onions, including tops, sliced thinly

1 to 1 1/2-inch slice of fresh ginger, julienned

1/2 cup canola oil

Instructions

Place fish in a flat pan in boiling water to poach. Thin orange roughy takes about 3 minutes; other fish, longer, depending upon thickness. Do not overcook.

Drain off water or lift fish to a heated platter.

Sprinkle green onions and ginger over fish. Pour soy sauce mixed with sesame oil over the fish, onions and ginger.

Heat the canola oil to almost "smoking." When you pour it over the fish, it will sizzle while it cooks the flavor of the other ingredients into the fish.

Delicious and fun to do the last step -- the "sizzling" part -- right at the table. Just make sure you follow Glen's advice so you don't send your guests running for cover!

Dr. Glen Egstrom is the Past President of the Los Angeles County Instructor Association, NAUI, and American Academy Underwater Seminars. He is also Professor Emeritus, Physiological Sciences Department UCLA, and Retired Captain of Los Angeles County Sheriff's Reserve Search and Rescue Unit.

Glen specializes in writing research papers for scientific journals on topics ranging from human factors and kinesiology to evaluations of diving and underwater equipment.

He co-authored the book, *Stress and Performance in Diving,* with Art Bachrach (see page 24).

Glen Egstrom has received the prestigious Leonard Greenstone Award for contributions to Diving Safety, the Our World - Underwater Award, the Underwater Society of America's coveted NOGI Award, and the Oceaneering International Award for Contributions to Man in the Sea.

He is currently the Diving Safety Officer, Los Angeles County Sheriff's Department, Chairman of the Board of Directors of the Our World - Underwater Scholarship Society, and Director of the UCLA Diving Safety Research Project.

Dan Wagner's
"FishyDan's" Delight

"I used to do a lot of spearfishing and ate a lot of yellowtail, hogfish and grouper. But I don't eat grouper any more. They are my friends ever since I made a video about fish behaviour called "Grouper Sex." Now I enjoy this recipe made with tilapia or farm-raised catfish. If you must eat a sea friend, fix it right."
-- Dan Wagner

Ingredients
Mayonnaise (can be fat-free)
Fish fillets, 1/2 lb. per person
Old Bay seasoning
Lime juice

Instructions
Lightly spread mayo on both sides of fish.
Heat pan on medium (#3 on my stove)
Sprinkle Old Bay on fillets.
Squeeze lime juice lightly on fillets
Cook 8 - 10 minutes.

Dan uses a George Foreman Grill, but the recipe works just fine in the broiler or on the barbecue. This is a great-tasting, low-fat recipe, and it doesn't mask the flavor of your freshly-caught fish!

Dan Wagner is a pioneer sport diver who began his diving career in the Chicago area in 1954 where he helped develop organized diving, YMCA scuba instruction, and the first dive clubs and councils in the Chicago area. He helped develop the first manual describing practical search patterns for the use of fire and police departments. He has certified over 5,000 divers.

He moved to Florida in 1963 where he led the quest for successful, safe live-aboard dive boats. He also began documenting historic shipwrecks in 1964 working with Mel Fisher, and has since captured on film and video some of the greatest treasure finds in history, including the discovery of the *Atocha* and the recoveries of the 1715 Plate Fleet and 1733 Plate Fleet off Florida's East Coast.

He expanded into television freelance shooting, with his material appearing on ABC, NBC, TNT, CNN, Westinghouse, TBS of Japan, and the BBC in England.

Dan took every opportunity to document his Sea Friends and was the first vessel owner to develop swimming with wild dolphins in the Bahamas in 1979. To bring more attention to the beauty of the oceans, he has produced music videos and fish identification videos. He shot and produced a film called "Grouper Sex" that helped initiate the first protection of grouper during their spawning seasons; this protection is expanding throughout the Caribbean. Presently Dan helped develop the Mother Ocean Foundation and will be doing a series of educational videos and CD-ROM storybooks for early elementary school children.

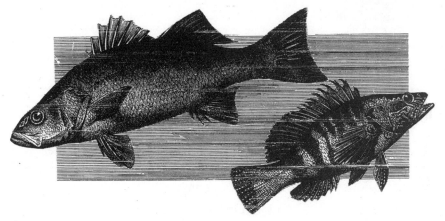

Dennis Gagnon's
Barbecued Narc-ed Fish

"I got this recipe from my next door neighbors, who own a liquor store (someone has to live next door to them). He was a chef before that!

"I am one who will barbecue any time of the year. For the softies who live in the warm year-round climates, that's the Midwest year. We will cook out even when it is 0 degrees. This recipe is a great one for New Year's Eve. You may have to increase the wine content (on the side) before the night is over." -- Dennis Gagnon.

Dennis tries to catch fish the hard way. Photo submitted by Dennis Gagnon.

Ingredients (serves 4)

2 lbs. white fish fillets

1/4 cup soy sauce

1/2 cup dry white wine

1 1/4 tablespoon fresh lemon juice

1 clove garlic, pressed

1/2 teaspoon ground ginger

1 tablespoon fresh rosemary

2 1/2 tablespoons fresh parsley

1/2 lb. mushrooms, sliced

1/3 cup butter or margarine

Instructions

Combine soy sauce, wine, lemon juice, garlic and ginger. Pour over fish pieces and marinate 4 hours. Make a pan from heavy-duty aluminum foil. Place fish in pan. Sprinkle with rosemary and parsley. Cover with another piece of foil. Be sure to save marinade!

Place over low coals and cook until fish flakes, about 10-15 minutes. It needs to flake easily when tested with a fork. Meanwhile, sauté mushrooms in butter, add remaining marinade and heat thoroughly. Pour over grilled fish and enjoy!

Do not go overboard (no pun intended) with the soy sauce, or it will spoil the dish.

* This is delicious, but if the snow has buried your outdoor grill, just cook it in your broiler and enjoy it in the winter.

Dennis Gagnon, a resident of Villa Park, Illinois, has been diving for 30 years and shooting underwater images for 25 years. His love of the ocean has taken him all over the world, including the Red Sea, Atlantic and Pacific Oceans plus the Great Lakes, with his most recent stops the Coral Sea and the Great Barrier Reef. He retired after 33 years from education, 7 years teaching and 26 years in school administration.

Photo submitted by Dennis Gagnon.

In 2000, he was recognized by the Council for Elementary Science International, a Division Affiliate of the National Science Teachers Association, as the Elementary Principal of the Year for his leadership in Science Education. Because of his love of science and the ocean, Dennis has given over 200 presentations to children from Early Childhood through high school. He has been one of several volunteer Directors of "Our World -- Underwater" for 23 years and OWU"s Program Director for 10 years.

Dan Lenihan's
Old Baywatch Delight (camping version)

"I learned this trick in association with the woman I eventually married because of her great culinary skills. I recommend secluded coves you can drive to around San Carlos, Mexico, on the Sea of Cortez to best enjoy this recipe. Good associated reading with this dish is John Steinbeck's *Log From the Sea of Cortez*." -- Dan Lenihan

Ingredients

Dead fish
Butter
Old Bay seasoning
Mexican salsa
Tequila

Lemon
Lime
Salt
Double sleeping bag

Instructions

Drive to secluded Mexican beach in company of attractive member of opposite sex (or same sex, matter of personal taste).

Unpack spear gun and shoot fish.

Place on left side, liberally smeared with butter (the fish in the pan, that is).

Sprinkle Old Bay seasoning on right side of fish. Add slices of lemon.

Cut lime and squeeze juice on base of thumb, add salt, lick thumb, lick partner's thumb, drink tequila, share sleeping bag.

Fish is ready when meat begins to flake easily from the bones -- if partner is ready, you will probably forget about the fish anyway.

*If you're very concerned about more specific instructions for creating this dish, you're not paying enough attention to the other elements for making this a perfect recipe for romance.

Dan Lenihan is an underwater archaeologist, the former Chief of the Submerged Cultural Resources Unit (SCRU) of the National Park Service. He spent 25 years supervising underwater archaeology projects in the Federal Government and is the U.S. delegate to the International Committee on Underwater Cultural heritage. He was the principal investigator of the underwater surveys of the USS *Arizona* in Pearl Harbor, the Isle Royale shipwreck study, Bikini Atoll resurvey of wrecks, and the 1996 documentation of the *H.L. Hunley,* the Confederate submarine. Dan and his SCRU team have been the subject of national media stories and numerous television documentaries on CBS, ABC, BBC, CNN, PBS, The Discovery and History Channels, and National Geographic.

Dan has maintained active status as a NAUI instructor since 1972 and was certified by NACD in 1993 as a cave diving instructor.

He is the author or editor of several books, among them

Dan Lenihan signs a copy of the book which he co-authored with actor Gene Hackman, who, pen in hand, awaits his turn.

Underwater Wonders of the National Parks (co-authored with John Brooks), the well-received sea adventure novel, *The Wake of the Perdido Star* (with co-author actor Gene Hackman), and, most recently, the critically acclaimed *Submerged: Adventures of America's Most Elite Underwater Archaeology Team.*

A native New Yorker and former schoolteacher, Dan lives with his family in Santa Fe, New Mexico.

Mike & Georgann Wachter's
Perfect Perch/Awesome Abalone

"The breading mix we first used on abalone when we lived in California. Since we had three kids under six years of age, it was difficult to get babysitters. We joined a club to get new buddies so one of us was left to babysit.

"This club mainly dove to hunt off the northern California shore. Mike would go out with a spearfishing buddy and spot ling cod for him to bag. Then I would free dive for abalone. Since I was not good at spotting these shellfish, the guys I went out with would pop an abalone off the rocks and attach it to my wetsuit so I could ferry it back to the rubber raft.

"We haven't seen too many abalone in the Great Lakes, so when you're hungry after diving, catch perch and use the same recipe." -- Mike & Georgann Wachter

Ingredients

Adapt ingredients to amount of seafood:

Fresh perch fillet or well-pounded abalone

Flour

Salt

Pepper

1 or 2 eggs

1 or 2 teaspoons Worcestershire sauce

Bread crumbs

1 or 2 tablespoons parsley

Vegetable oil

Instructions

Mix flour with salt and pepper in one bowl.

Prepare a second bowl mixture of 1 or 2 eggs beaten with 1 or 2 teaspoons Worcestershire sauce.

Have a third mixture of bread crumbs and 1 or 2 tablespoons parsley.

Dredge perch or abalone first in flour mix, then dip in egg mixture. Finally coat with bread crumbs.

Pan or deep fry in vegetable oil for 30 seconds to 1 minute per side till fork tender.

*This is a very good recipe for frying not just perch and abalone, but other kinds of fish as well. Experiment! And while you're at it, try it with Wes Skiles' "'Hey Now!' Special Sauce" (see page 68).

Mike & Georgann Wachter, the authors of three Lake Erie shipwreck books since 1997, *Erie Wrecks, Erie Wrecks East* and *Erie Wrecks West,* have been diving around the world since the early 1970's. They discovered diving while snorkeling in the Mediterranean Sea in 1972 during a backpacking trip through Europe. Since that time, they have visited many sites in the Caribbean, Atlantic, Pacific and Great Lakes.

However, nowhere else in the world have they discovered the kind of pristine and perfectly preserved shipwrecks that lie in the fresh waters of the Great Lakes. Living near Lake Erie led to the fascination with Lake Erie shipwrecks that drove the extensive research effort that is exhibited in their three books. Georgann is an accomplished researcher who is sought after as a speaker on sport diving, Great Lakes shipwrecks and aquatic life. She has had the opportunity to have her marine artwork exhibited around the Great Lakes. Mike makes his living as a business consultant and public speaker. He has written a business book, *Eight Lies of Teamwork*.

Submitted by Mike and Georgann Wachter.

Robert Marx's
"For Treasure and Pleasure" Sea Bass

"This recipe is inspired by a dish at Atlanta's wonderful restaurant, The Atlanta Fish Market." -- Bob Marx

"Our daughter, Hilary, and her husband, John Gregory, had their engagement party there. This recipe is the result of my efforts to duplicate their sea bass dish. Since sea bass is now on the endangered list and eating it is not PC [politically correct], I suggest listing halibut and cod as alternatives for the recipe. Bob and I lecture on Princess Cruise Lines and have been in Chile recently several times and have seen how there, they are still catching and exporting sea bass and even selling it locally but hypocritically calling it 'sea eel'!!!" -- Jenifer Marx

Ingredients (for 4 persons)

2 lbs. Chilean sea bass, skinned

1/2 cup low sodium soy sauce

1/4 cup sugar (optional)

1/2 cup medium-dry sherry

4 fat garlic cloves, peeled and smashed

2 tablespoons fresh lime juice (or lemon juice)

1 tablespoon minced scallion

2 tablespoons toasted sesame seeds

6 slices fresh ginger root

1 1/2 lbs. fresh spinach, steamed (or use 2-3 boxes frozen whole-leaf spinach)

Instructions

Combine soy, sugar and sherry in a glass measuring cup or bowl and heat one minute in microwave until sugar dissolves. Add garlic and ginger. Marinate fish in one-half of mixture for 30 minutes or so. Bring remaining sauce to a boil on stove and reduce to about 1/3 cup. Remove garlic and ginger and stir in lime juice and sesame seeds. Set aside.

Steam, grill or broil fish until done (8 - 10 minutes per inch of thickness). Remove to 4 dinner plates which have a mound of spinach on them and top with the sauce and chopped scallions.

This is absolutely delicious -- the sauce is intense, but just relax and let your eyes roll heavenward. It doesn't overpower the fish because sea bass is robust enough to stand up to it.

Robert F. Marx, an adventurer-explorer in the grand style,is one of the most successful and well-known specialists in the field of marine archaeology, and he has an equally strong reputation for his work in naval and maritime history and treasure salvage. The author of over 40 books and approximately 700 scientific reports and popular articles since the 1950's, Bob writes with enthusiasm, clarity and a sense of humor usually absent in that genre. He left his native Pittsburgh at the age of 13, first explored the underwater world of Lake St.

Clair from a cousin's cottage along the Canadian shoreline, spent three years in the U.S. Marine Corps, was in charge of the USMC diving school where he trained over 5,000 Marines in scuba diving and amphibious warfare, and operated the first scuba dive shop in Cozumel. Early in his career, he found a number of Spanish and English shipwrecks from the period 1650-1800 off the coasts of Puerto Rico and the Virgin Islands, discovered Mayan temple sites in Mexico, explored ancient Phoenician seaports in Lebanon, and was knighted by the Queen of Spain.

Sir Robert has discovered and excavated ancient shipwrecks in over 60 countries, and he has produced or shot over 50 documentary films.

Jenifer Grant Marx is a writer interested in history and underwater archaeology. A graduate of Mount Holyoke College, she also studied history at the University of Florence in Italy. She was a member of the first U.S. Peace Corps contingent, serving in the Philippines from 1961 to 1963 where she worked on the islands of Negros and Mindanao. She subsequently lived in Europe, Africa, the West Indies and Asia.

Jenifer, also a diver, historian and writer, met future husband Bob in Jamaica, where she assisted him in his four-year excavation of the sunken city of Port Royal. They have co-authored several books as a team. They have three daughters and live in Indiatlantic on Florida's east-central coast when either or both of them are not traveling over the world.

Dick Boyd's
Campfire Whitefish

"Fifty years ago, every Great Lakes port town, large or small, had a local fishery where seafood could be readily purchased. Divers, camping in remote places while searching for shipwrecks, often created fine campsite cuisine with fresh fish. Campfire Whitefish was a big favorite then and remains so today!" -- Dick Boyd

Ingredients

Large whitefish fillets (one per healthy appetite)

Lemon wedges and thick onion slices

Creamy Italian salad dressing

Butter pats

Seasonings

Sliced new potatoes

Carrots (optional)

Instructions

Wash the fillets and wrap in aluminum foil. Garnish generously with lemon and onion slices. Add a liberal coating of Italian dressing and several pats of butter. Season to taste.

Cook over a low fire, turning once, allowing about 8 to 12 minutes per side, depending upon the condition of the coals. Done when fish is moist and flaky. (Sliced potatoes and carrots can be included or wrapped and cooked separately).

Very good and very easy. Squeeze the hot lemon over the fish when done -- don't burn your fingers!

Richard J. Boyd, Ph.D. in microbiology and oceanography, has been an active diver since 1954, specializing in shipwreck, TEK and commercial diving, including underwater demolition. He has been a PADI Instructor for 30 years and is founding member #13 of that agency. He worked as an

associate diver for the *Alvin Clark* Salvage, as well as for the Wisconsin Underwater Archaeology Program, Sea Grant, and National Park Service projects. He has also worked as a Sea Grant Project Reviewer and as Chairman of the State of Wisconsin's Submerged Cultural Resource Advisory Council. He is a Director of the Wisconsin Underwater Archaeology Association and an instructor for underwater archaeology courses. Currently he is Technical Director of Global Manufacturing Corporation, a major producer of SCUBA test apparatus and gas mixing equipment.

FOURTH COURSE: LANDLUBBER ENTRÉES

""The boat food that I like to take is C-rations, and it has a couple of different advantages. One is that if you don't eat it that day, it doesn't go bad. It's not like cold cuts. You have to throw the sandwich out at the end of the day....You have to develop a taste for it. I've had 20-year-old C-rations that I took on the boat and if I didn't eat them that day, I just took them the next week, and I just kept using them all summer long. The other advantage is that I did offer to share my lunch with other people. They all declined. So I didn't have to share any of my food with anyone, and I still got brownie points for offering." -- Gary Gentile [see page 18 for Gary's recipe.]

You see, divers do not live by seafood alone. And, according to Ernie Brooks [for his recipe, see page 56], photographers normally do not eat their subjects. Check out these land-based dishes:

DAVE TROTTER's **Road Kill Venison Stew** .... page 84

VRENI RODUNER's **Chicken in Cream Sauce** .... page 86

JEFF GRAY's **Beer Butt Chicken** .... page 88

VALERIE OLSON VAN HEEST's **Sterts** .... page 90

JESSE CANCELMO's **Flower Gardens Eggplant Parmigiana** .... page 92

KARL HUGGINS' **Rapid Ascent Spaghetti Sauce** .... page 94

JONATHAN BIRD's **Stuffed Shells and Garlic Bread** .... page 96

JIM & PAT STAYER's **Too-Many-Divers-in-the-House Chili** .... page 98

RALPH WHITE's **Mixed Gas Chili & Beans ("Titanic" version)** .. page 100

MIKE WILLIAMS' **Zesty Mariner's Meatloaf** .... page 102

STAN WATERMAN's **Peerless Meatloaf** .... page 104

EMORY KRISTOFF's **"Red Meat Diver's" Steak** .... page 106

HAL WATTS' **Steak To Dive For** .... page 108

JIM BOWDEN's **Steak and Seduction** .... page 110

BOB SANDERS' **South Pole-ish Pork** .... page 112

ANN KRISTOVICH's **Smokin' Ribs** .... page 114

Dave Trotter's
Road Kill Venison Stew

"Jeff Moore, for whom the recipe 'Road Kill Venison Stew' is named, will go to any extreme to obtain venison. There are a couple of ways of obtaining the 'Road Kill.' One method he employed very successfully was to have one of the team members drive his recently purchased truck down the road, and Jeff followed. When the deer ran in front of the truck (causing several $1,000's in damage), Jeff immediately jumped out of his 'older' vehicle and finished the task of getting the deer ready for the boat. On more than one occasion, Jeff has obtained 'Road Kill' venison while traveling to and from search/dive expeditions, thereby keeping this 'lowlife' crew of never-do-wells adequately fed." -- Dave Trotter

Ingredients (serves 4)

3 lbs. of venison (or substitute boneless chicken breast)

3 tablespoons of flour

1/4 teaspoon of garlic powder

1 tablespoon of cooking oil

chopped clove of garlic

1 4-ounce can of sliced mushrooms, drained

1 small onion

1 lb. can of chopped tomatoes and juice

1 cup dry white wine or white sherry cooking wine (beer works, too)

4 cups of hot cooked rice

Instructions

Season and flour the meat and brown it on both sides in hot oil.

In a 3 1/2-to-4 quart slow cooker, place the sliced onion and add meat.

Add other ingredients except for half the wine.

Cook on high for 4 1/2 to 5 hours, or low heat setting for 10-12 hours.

Add rest of wine after cooking is done. Serve over rice.

For 6 servings, add 1 more pound of meat and cook in 5-6 quart cooker.

Cooking setting and time are determined by the weather and the estimated time that the shipwreck search will end and the crew returns.

This dish makes delicious smells in the kitchen all day and is so easy to make! The flavor of the sauce permeates the meat which is fall-apart tender.

David L. Trotter has worked at discovering virgin shipwrecks -- more than 80 of them in four of the five Great Lakes, a feat which ranks him at the lead among underwater sleuths of the inland seas.

He has written several articles on Great Lakes Shipwrecks which have been

published in historical journals and in national scuba diving publications in both Canada and the United States.

The multi-media programs he develops out of his expeditions, making diving into history come alive, are featured at film festivals and on television. He has been featured in many publications about shipwrecks over the past 25 years.

Vreni Roduner's
Chicken in Cream Sauce

"The Scalloped Chicken in Cream Sauce I often make to bring to someone's home, then reheat it quickly. It became a tradition in some homes. It is easy to make, but at first glance you may think it is complicated. It is a well-liked derivation of a Swiss National Dish, generally made with veal.

"Bon appetit. Enjoy!" -- Vreni Roduner

Ingredients (serves 3 - 4)

1 lb. prepared chicken breasts

2-3 tablespoons olive oil for sautéeing

2 teaspoons flour

1 tablespoon lemon juice

1/4 teaspoon paprika

1 teaspoon salt

1 small onion, minced

10-12 oz. fresh white mushrooms -- wash in the last minute, slice then toss with 1 tablespoon fresh lemon juice

1/2 cup dry white wine

1/2 - 3/4 cup heavy cream

Instructions

Heat oil in frying pan -- pat sliced chicken dry with a paper towel -- do in portions.

Dust with flour and quickly sauté with high heat. Put into deep dish.

Sprinkle with the seasoning and lemon juice, toss and cover.

Put 1 teaspoon oil into the frying pan. Add the onions. Stir.

Add sliced mushrooms, toss and sauté until done (2 to 3 minutes).

Add onion/mushroom mixture to the chicken, but not the liquid. Keep the liquid in the pan.

Pour the wine into the hot liquid, and simmer until reduced by half.

Add cream and simmer to thicken a bit (1 to 2 minutes)

Add chicken mixture to sauce, stir, add freshly ground pepper to taste.

Reheat quickly and serve.

Serve with good curly noodles, or "Spatzle" or "Swiss Rosti" -- shredded home fries with finely-diced onions, browned to a golden 'pancake' and a big mixed salad.

This is easy to make and has a delicate flavor, sure to please everyone.

Vreni Roduner learned to dive in 1974 and became the first female divemaster of The Scuba Sports Club (New York) in 1980.

In 1986, she participated in Repex, a NOAA-sponsored saturation excursion program for the purpose of predicting the longterm effects of oxygen exposure.

She is the recipient of the Beneath The Sea Medal of Excellence and their 20-Year Award for loyalty and dedicated service, as well as the Scuba Sports Club Diver of the Year Award. Vreni was also a participant in the Aqua Women expeditions from 1981 to 1993.

She is an inaugural member of the Women Divers Hall of Fame.

Photo submitted by Vreni Roduner.

Jeff Gray's
Beer Butt Chicken

"This is a traditional Wisconsin Archaeological Field School recipe. It was everyone's favorite when we were doing field work in Door County." -- Jeff Gray

Ingredients

1 whole chicken

Hickory dry rub

1 can of beer (I recommend Leinenkugel's)

Hickory wood chips

Instructions

Soak the hickory wood chips with half a can of beer (overnight if you have the time).

Rub the whole chicken with hickory dry rub (lots of it).

Add 2 teaspoons of hickory dry rub to the remaining can of beer and insert beer can into the chicken. Make sure the neck is sealed closed with toothpicks to keep beer steam from escaping.

Place chicken upright on grill and slow cook for 4 hours. If you don't have 4 hours, you can cut the time a bit. Check for doneness. Throughout cooking, place wood chips around the chicken.

Jeff Gray shows how a single chicken/beer combo should look when it sits over the fire for four hours.

*This is a sure-fire fun party dish. Everyone will love the hilarious sight of chickens lined up "sitting" on cans, waiting to be dinner!

Jeff Gray is the manager of the Thunder Bay National Marine Sanctuary and Underwater Preserve. Jeff has a strong background in research, management, and protection. Serving as State Underwater Archaeologist at the Wisconsin Historical Society since 1998, he managed a statewide cultural resource program and developed and implemented the Wisconsin Maritime Trails system. He also acted as a scientific diver and lab technician for NOAA's National Undersea Research Center in Key Largo, Florida, in addition to conducting other archaeological work in North Carolina, Wisconsin, the Dominican Republic, Chile and Greece. Jeff also has extensive experience developing partnerships among and working with government agencies, businesses, non-profit organizations, and user groups. In particular, he worked with these entities to interpret Wisconsin's maritime history and preserve underwater archaeological sites.

Jeff, an Our World - Underwater Scholarship winner, has published numerous

Jeff Gray poses proudly with one of the large, plastic buoys which will mark the shipwrecks in the new NOAA Sanctuary in Lake Huron at Alpena, Michigan.

articles in the field of Great Lakes underwater archaeology. He serves on numerous associated boards and committees. He received a B.A. in Anthropology and Archaeology from Wisconsin's Beloit College and a M.A. in Maritime History and Underwater Archaeology from North Carolina's East Carolina University.

Valerie Olson Van Heest's
Sterts

Valerie strikes a Great Lakes scuba diver's version of a 'Victoria's Secret'-style pose.

"This recipe was passed down from my maternal grandmother. It was made regularly in Austria especially for skiers because it is nourishing, it stays with you a long time, and it gives you strength. Some skiers even carry it cold in a pouch for a quick burst of energy on the slopes. I remember waking up to the wonderful aroma of Sterts (pronounced 'shtehrts') on Sunday mornings as a kid and really appreciating the effort my Dad had made to cook my favorite breakfast. And when I grew up and became a diver, I realized that Sterts is not for skiers only! We divers, who bundle up in our thermal underwear and drysuits and descend into the cold, clear waters of the Great Lakes, need energy and stamina, too! That makes it a perfect morning meal for divers also!" -- Valerie Olson Van Heest

Ingredients (serves up to 8 people)

1 - 24 ounce container of Quaker
    yellow cornmeal
2 sticks of butter

Salt
Boiling water

Instructions

It's easy, but it takes about an hour!

Boil 2 quarts of water. In a separate bowl, mix the cornmeal with 1 teaspoon of salt. Heat a large frying pan to low and slowly melt 1 1/2 sticks of butter in the pan.

Slowly pour the cornmeal into the frying pan, mixing it thoroughly with the melted butter. Then add the boiling water into the cornmeal mixture in the frying pan, mixing it with a wooden spoon. You will have to add the water slowly and judge for yourself the proper amount. The consistency should be lumpy and paste-like. Cover the frying pan and cook on low-medium heat for about 10 minutes. Uncover and, using your wooden spoon, push cornmeal towards the middle of pan away from edges, creating a small lump in the middle.

Then add about 8 pats of butter around the edges of the cornmeal, using your remaining half stick of butter. This butter will help form the crust. Reduce the temperature just above low, re-cover and let cook for about 45 minutes. Don't turn the heat up too high, as it is easy to burn the cornmeal! Check the cornmeal a couple of times. Lift the forming crust and make sure it is not sticking to pan or burning. Adjust temperature if necessary. Taste it as it cooks and add salt if necessary. You can also add boiling water if the mixture is too granular. Before serving, fluff the cornmeal around the entire pan, and break the crust into smaller pieces.

Serve warm in bowls, making sure each person gets some fluffy cornmeal and crust (I think the crust is the best part!) Some people eat it salted; some like it with syrup. It is a simple, filling and tasty breakfast treat. Don't be afraid to make too much, as it is great heated in the microwave for leftovers.

*This is a stick-to-the-ribs comfort food and reminds me of corn meal mush, a traditional Southern U.S. favorite. A non-stick pan is helpful for this recipe.

Valerie Olson Van Heest has been involved in shipwreck research and documentation projects for the past 12 of her 22-year diving "career," which began when, as a teenager, she worked for Dacor Corporation. As an Architectural Project Manager, Valerie utilizes her drawing and management skills in her avocational pursuits in Underwater Archaeology.

Valerie served as Director of the Underwater Archaeological Society of Chicago (UASC), where for 8 years, she and fellow UASC members conducted projects on 20 Chicago-area shipwrecks, including the *Seabird, Lady Elgin* and *Wells Burt,* all resulting in reports and slide presentations. She also worked on joint venture projects on shipwrecks in Lake Huron (the *Goshawk*), Lake Erie and Biscayne Bay, Florida.

In 1995, she married a Michigan man, Jack Van Heest, who is also a diver, relocated to West Olive, Michigan, and became President of the

Valerie with survey marker tags which were placed onto artifacts on Lake Huron's *Goshawk* shipwreck.

Southwest Michigan Underwater Preserve, a state underwater preserve designation which became official in 1999. Valerie has documented four of the Preserve's shipwrecks, organized an ongoing search for the elusive wreck of the *Chicora* (West Michigan's most enigmatic maritime mystery), and directed "The *Verano*, A Porthole to the Past," a grant project from the Michigan Humanities Council.

Valerie works for GMB Architects - Engineers in Holland, Michigan.

Jesse Cancelmo's
Flower Gardens Eggplant Parmigiana

"When I was single, I had a girlfriend from New York who I thought made the best eggplant parmigiana in the universe. That honor now goes to my wife, Christine." -- Jesse Cancelmo

Ingredients

2 small eggplants, peeled

2 cups of ricotta cheese

1/4 cup grated parmesan cheese

2 eggs

1/2 cup olive oil

2 cups tomato sauce

1/2 pound grated mozzarella cheese

Salt and black pepper, to taste

Instructions

Slice eggplant into 1/2-inch pieces, layer in colander, salt lightly.

Mix eggs, ricotta and parmesan cheeses. Season with salt and pepper.

Heat 2 tablespoons of olive oil in skillet and add eggplant slices. Fry until brown both sides. Remove to paper towels and drain.

Spread 1/2 cup tomato sauce on bottom of gratin dish, arrange eggplant slices and top each with a tablespoon of ricotta, some tomato sauce and sprinkle mozzarella over top. Repeat layers of eggplant slices, adding ricotta, tomato sauce and mozzarella, end with sauce on top.

Pre-heat oven to 400 degrees F. and bake for 25-30 minutes.

Let stand for 10 minutes before serving.

*This is a wonderful traditional Italian dish. Incidentally, it was named after the tropical reef popular with divers in the northern part of the Gulf of Mexico. Serve this Eggplant Parmigiana with Karl Huggins' Rapid Ascent Spaghetti Sauce [see page 94] and Jonathan Bird's Stuffed Shells and Garlic Bread, and you'll have a magnificent Italian feast! Mangia! Mangia!

Jesse Cancelmo is an Italian-American underwater photographer based in Houston, Texas. He specializes in Flower Gardens and Eggplant Parmigiana.

A native of Philadelphia, Jesse was scuba certified in 1970 and cut his teeth on Jersey wreck diving in the early '70's. He relocated to Houston in 1976 where he remains active in the local dive community. Jesse is a PADI Divemaster and was recently certified as a technical trimix diver (TDI). In October, 1999, he dived the famous Civil War ship, *U.S.S. Monitor,* located off the coast of North Carolina in 230 feet of water.

Photo submitted by Jesse Cancelmo.

He is an accomplished underwater photographer, author and photojournalist. His articles and photographs have appeared in numerous diving and wildlife publications. He has authored two books, *Diving Bermuda* (1990) and *Diving Cayman Islands* (1998). Jesse is a contributing writer/photographer for *Dive Training Magazine*, and he leads groups on Caribbean and Pacific dive adventures.

Karl Huggins'
Rapid Ascent Spaghetti Sauce

"This recipe was mutated from my mother's recipe for spaghetti and meatballs, since I didn't have enough time to do it properly in college." -- Karl Huggins

Ingredients

1/2 pound chunk of ground beef or turkey

Onion -- sliced very thin

Garlic -- at least 3 buds, sliced very thin

Red wine

Butter

Olive oil

1 small can tomato paste

1 medium can tomato sauce

Basil

Oregano

Dash of sugar

Pasta

Instructions

Brown ground beef/turkey in olive oil in cast iron skillet. Set aside.

Sauté onions and garlic in butter in same skillet.

When onions are transparent, add enough red wine to cover onions and garlic, add beef/turkey, sprinkle thin layer of oregano over it, sprinkle twice as much basil, and let simmer for about a minute.

Add tomato paste and mix together well. Add tomato sauce to thin it out, and throw in a dash of sugar. Bring to bubble, stirring, then reduce to low for as long as you want.

Use with any pasta you like.

This smelled so good, and it drove the editor's husband crazy. This recipe goes well with Jonathan Bird's stuffed shells (see page 96).

Karl Huggins began diving in 1977 and became a NAUI Instructor in 1980. He has been the Program Manager for the Catalina Hyperbaric Chamber Facility at the USC Wrigley Marine Science Center since 1992.

He is noted for his work in decompression theory and models, which resulted in the Michigan Sea Grant (HUGI) tables and his participation in the development of the EDGE dive computer in the 1980's.

He has given over 100 lectures, workshops and conferences around the world, authored publications on decompression theory, including, most recently, "The Dynamics of Decompression Workbook," and contributed to "Dive Computers - A Consumer's Guide to History, Theory and Performance."

Karl is the 1990 recipient of the Leonard Greenstone Diving Safety Award and the DAN/Rolex Diver of the Year for 1993.

Jonathan Bird's
Stuffed Shells and Garlic Bread

First, Jonathan's Stuffed Shells

"This stuffed shell recipe is pretty easy (after all, I can make it!) and no innocent sea creatures get hurt! [See Ernie Brooks' comment on page 83.] This recipe is guaranteed to impress women." -- Jonathan Bird

Ingredients

1 box of large shells (12 oz.)

1 large jar of spaghetti sauce, 16 oz. (I prefer Prego with mushrooms, but sometimes I substitute my wife's homemade sauce when available)

2 pounds of ricotta cheese -- not the wimpy low-fat stuff either!

2 eggs, beaten somewhat

1/2 cup powdered Parmesan cheese (the kind you put on spaghetti)

Shredded mozzarella cheese

1 tablespoon basil

1 tablespoon oregano

Instructions

Bring a large pot of water to a boil and toss the shells in there carefully to avoid breaking them. Stir frequently or they will stick to the bottom of the pot. Cook until tender and not crunchy in the middle. Hint: If you test one, don't throw it back into the pot with an obvious bite taken out of it!

In a large mixing bowl (better yet, in a large mixer), add the ricotta cheese, eggs, Parmesan cheese, basil and oregano. Mix it until well combined.

Drain and strain the cooked shells in a colander and allow to cool. I like to speed the process by putting them back into the pot, filling with cold water and straining again. Important safety tip: if you try to stuff the shells without allowing them to cool, you will burn yourself!

Pour some of the spaghetti sauce into a large (9x12) baking pan. You need just enough to cover the bottom of the pan. This should be about 1/4 of the jar.

Using a spoon, stuff each shell with cheese mixture. Yes, it's a pain. Just do it and quit complaining. Arrange stuffed shells in the pan in a tight pattern.

Once all the shells are finished, dump the rest of the sauce onto them to cover everything. Sprinkle the top with shredded mozzarella. Cover with aluminum foil (careful, don't let the foil touch the cheese on top or it will stick) and bake at 350 for about 45 minutes.

Serve with garlic bread, red wine and candles. Flowers on the table help, too. You are on your way to a good first impression! Let me know how you do.

Second, Jonathan's Easy Garlic Bread

"If you're making my stuffed shells, or any other Italian dish for that matter, you better have some good garlic bread. Not just any garlic bread will do. Garlic bread is easy, so pay attention...."
-- Jonathan Bird

Ingredients

1 loaf of French bread

Soft margarine (the kind in a tub). Use real margarine, not those fake bread spreads. If you use the wrong thing, your bread will taste funny. There's nothing wrong with margarine. Just use it!

Garlic powder

Garlic salt

Instructions

Proper bread is the long and skinny kind, like a Navy submarine. Cut it into sections which are 4 inches long, then cut each section into two pieces, top and bottom, as if you were making a sandwich out of them.

Lay out a long piece of aluminum foil on a flat cookie sheet. Lay each matched pair of bread pieces on the aluminum foil. Spread a thin layer of margarine on each piece of bread. Then sprinkle each piece with garlic powder and garlic salt. The salt is very important. Without the salt, the bread has no flavor. If you don't use garlic salt, use a little extra garlic powder and substitute regular table salt for the garlic salt.

Put each matched pair of bread pieces back together, wrap the whole thing in the foil and toss it in the oven for the last 10 minutes with your stuffed shells (that's about 10 minutes at 350 degrees).

Photo submitted by Jonathan Bird.

These recipes are good and easy to make. The addition of herbs (especially fresh) to the cheese is a nice flavorful touch. Be careful not to overcook the shells or they won't be shells any more, just little pieces of pasta! Why not use Karl Huggins' Rapid Ascent Spaghetti Sauce (doubled) with this? See page 94.

Jonathan Bird is a professional underwater photographer and President of the non-profit organization Oceanic Research Group, Inc. He has filmed and produced many educational films about marine life and ocean ecosystems for use in schools. He shot and produced "Sharks: The Real Story" for PBS in 1996 and "Beneath the North Atlantic" in 1998. He has won two Emmy awards for his underwater cinematography and production work in television. He has shot on assignment for many U.S. television networks and programs.

Jim & Pat Stayer's
Too-Many-Divers-in-the-House Chili

"We love to have our friends join us for diving off our charter boat, *Wildkat*. So every weekend during diving season, diver friends of ours show up at our house, sleeping bags in tow. We cook for an army (we all know how divers love to eat) and have great times. You have to be careful where you step if you get up in the middle of the night because it is wall-to-wall sleeping bags! This chili recipe was developed because we can make it the day before and then just re-heat it after a day of diving on fantastically preserved Lake Huron shipwrecks, and the army of divers comes back to our house, tired, wet and hungry, but happy." -- Jim & Pat Stayer

Ingredients

3 pounds ground chuck

1/2 bunch of celery

1 medium white onion

2 bell peppers -- 1 red, 1 green

1 lb. white mushrooms

1/2 head of garlic

1 tablespoon ground black pepper

3 tablespoons Lawry's seasoned salt

1 tablespoon Worcestershire sauce

2 gallon cans of tomato sauce

2 tablespoons parsley flakes

1 large can kidney beans

3 to 8 tablespoons ground cumin (to taste)

Tabasco sauce

Instructions

Finely chop the fresh vegetables. Brown the ground beef and drain off the grease.

Add the vegetables, tomato sauce, beans and seasonings. Bring to a boil.

Then simmer for 3 to 4 hours.

Serve with Tabasco sauce to taste.

This chili is better the second day and has been known to feed 12 divers, with some left over, and no complaints.

*My husband Cris and I have been fortunate to be part of the "army of divers" that the Stayers have opened their home, their boat and their hearts to. These diving weekends are all about great diving, great friends, and great food like this chili. Remember, divers love to eat, and divers love to eat garlic. That's why you'll never see any vampires on board the Wildkat!

Jim and Pat Stayer have been diving for 28 years and hold a number of advanced ratings. Respected historians, they are co-authors of *Shipwrecks of Sanilac* and *Sole Survivor,* and a number of videos on Great Lakes ship-wrecks.

Pat at the wheel of a tug which she helped locate, the *Mary Alice B.*, in 98 feet of Lake Huron water.

Jim has been a licensed U.S. Coast Guard Captain for the last 18 years, and along with Pat, runs a dive charter boat out of Lexington, Michigan.

Pat is a marine artist and computer graphics professional. Jim is the Past President of the Michigan Underwater Preserve Council, and both he and Pat are on the Board of Directors for the Lake Huron Shipwreck and Maritime Center.

Their goal is to locate and video shipwrecks so that others can enjoy "taking a step back in time." Their group has discovered and documented eight new shipwrecks in the Great Lakes.

Currently, Jim teaches television production and Pat is an elementary school teacher.

Jim & Pat Stayer and Cris Kohl [see page 36] sign their books at New York's Beneath The Sea's Ocean Pals booth.

Ralph White's
Mixed Gas Chili & Beans ("Titanic" Version)

"For many years, I competed in the California Chili Contest at Ghost Town Gold Mine in Antelope Valley. Two of us always shared top honors, alternating first and second prizes: I and C.G. Woods, President of McCullick Oil and married to actress Joanne Dru. We dressed up like cowboys and had great fun. I would send my chili out to friends as Christmas presents and traditionally served it after scuba diving." -- Ralph White

Ingredients (for 8 hungry divers)

1 whole chicken

3 beef soup broth bones

2 lbs. of sirloin steak

1 lb. of ground beef

1 lb. salt pork

8 large green or yellow chili peppers
    (12 for REAL divers)

8 tomatoes

3 onions

2 cloves of garlic

1 or 2 lbs. of pinto or chile beans

salt

pepper

celery salt

chili powder

crushed oregano

1 bottle of dark Mexican beer

Instructions

Boil the whole chicken and the beef soup bones for 1 to 2 hours. Drain the broth into a large pot (leaving a little chicken meat and some beef bone marrow with the broth is a personal choice) and let cool.

Finely dice 1 pound of salt pork and stir fry in pan until slightly crisp. Add fried salt pork to the broth, but leave the grease. Dice the 2 pounds of sirloin steak into small cubes. Fry in the pork grease till brown and add to broth.

Stir fry the 1 pound of chopped ground beef until browned and then add everything to the broth.

Steam or boil the 8 to 12 chili peppers until the natural wax hardens, then peel the wax off, finely dice and add to broth. Puree 5 tomatoes and add to the pot.

Finely dice 3 tomatoes, 2 garlic, and 3 onions, add to the broth and cook slowly over a low fire for 2 hours.

In a separate pot, cook 1 to 2 pounds of pinto or chili beans in a little virgin oil and water and salt for 2 1/2 to 3 hours until soft. Drain water and add beans to the chili base.

Add salt, pepper, celery salt, oregano, and chili powder to personal taste and simmer for 2 hours. (If you like your chili thicker, puree some of the beans).

Allow to cool and add 1 bottle of Mexican dark beer and place in refrigerator overnight.

Heat and serve after the dive, <u>NOT</u> <u>BEFORE</u>, especially if using a dry suit!

*This recipe will change the way you feel about chili -- it is really unique and deeply flavored. It's easy to see why this fabulous chili is a prizewinner.

Ralph White enjoys a distinguished professional career as an award-winning cinematographer, video cameraman, and editor with over 30 years of production experience and hundreds of motion picture and television credits.

Ralph is one of the few experienced people in the methods and technologies required to safely reach deep ocean depths to acquire images. In 1985, he documented the expedition that found the wreck of the *R.M.S. Titanic*, and in 1987, he co-directed the salvage operation and photography during the recovery of over 1,400 artifacts from the *Titanic's* debris field. He was the submersible cameraman for the 1991 IMAX feature film *Titanica*, and in 1995 was the expedition leader and a second unit cameraman for Jim Cameron's 20th Century Fox feature, *Titanic*. White holds the record for the most number of dives to the 12,000-foot-deep wreck of the *Titanic*, and has qualified as a co-pilot of the French Nautile and Russian Mir submersibles.

Ralph White poses for his 33rd submersible dive to the wreck of the *Titanic*. Photograph submitted by Ralph White.

For over 25 years, Ralph has served as a contract cameraman for the National Geographic Society, where he and staff photographer Emory Kristoff pioneered the development of advanced remote cameras, 3-D video, H.D.T.V., and deep ocean imaging and lighting systems. He has been to both Poles, and filmed the 156-year-old wreck of the *H.M.S. Breadalbane* under the Arctic ice cap. His cinematography has won numerous awards.

He is a highly qualified helicopter and astrovision aerial specialist, a Fellow in the Explorers Club and a Past President of the Adventurers' Club.

Mike Williams'
Zesty Mariner's Meatloaf

"My dive buddy, Phil Rafferty, and I spent many weekends camping and staying in various hotels as we explored Great Lakes shipwrecks in eastern Lake Ontario and the Upper St. Lawrence River. Now, Phil is probably the best model and dive buddy an underwater photographer could ever ask for. On our diving trips, we always brought our own food supply and shared our resources back and forth.

Mike (right) and Phil doing typical Canadian Great Lakes diving. Photo submitted by Mike Williams.

"On one occasion while we were diving out of Point Traverse with Ducks Divers, we decided to stay a few days past our planned departure due to the clear weather and amazing late fall visibility. After a day diving on the wreck of the *Olive Branch* and getting some of the best vis we had ever seen, we ended up back at our cottage and discovered we had very little food left. The nearest town and any stores were at least 45 minutes drive away, so we decided to combine what we had left. All we had was a package of hamburger, some breadcrumbs, some spices and a little ketchup. We borrowed a few more ingredients from Sue of Ducks Divers and, in a short time, we had our first batch of Zesty Mariner's Meatloaf. Several trips later and after some heated debate, we had our final version of our late fall Great Lakes delicacy. Oh yeah, those pictures we took that day were probably the best I have taken to date on a Great Lakes shipwreck. This recipe and those pictures would not exist if it were not for a great dive buddy to make it all happen." -- Mike Williams

Ingredients (makes 4-6 good-sized servings)

1 can (8 oz.) spaghetti sauce

1/4 cup brown sugar

1/4 cup vinegar

1 teaspoon mustard

1 egg, beaten

1 pkg. dry onion soup mix

1/4 cup bread crumbs

2 lbs. ground beef

1 1/2 teaspoons salt

1/4 teaspoon pepper

Instructions

In a bowl, combine sauce, brown sugar, vinegar and mustard, and set aside for later.

Beat egg in a large bowl, add onion soup mix, bread crumbs, ground beef, salt, and pepper. Add 1/2 cup of the sauce mixture and blend thoroughly. Place into a loaf pan.

Cook at 350 degrees F. for 45 minutes, then spoon 4-5 spoonfuls over the meatloaf. Put back in for another 15 minutes. Warm the rest of the sauce on the stove. Serve with rice or potatoes, with the rest of the sauce to top them.

This meatloaf is full of flavor and cuts nicely for sandwiches the next day!

Mike Williams, born and raised in Lindsay, Ontario, in the heart of cottage country, fell in love with the underwater world while watching "The Undersea World of Jacques Cousteau." He spent his early years snorkeling in local lakes and rivers where he searched for fishing lures and golf balls and watched the freshwater fish life. As soon as he turned 18, he took his basic scuba training and did his checkout dives in April in an ice-filled river. The next few years were spent diving in local lakes.

In 1983, he signed up for a commercial diving course north of Toronto and, when he finished, attended the College of Oceaneering in Los Angeles, California, where he trained as Diver Medical Technician. He then operated a Hyperbaric Chamber outside Toronto for two years before entering a law enforcement career.

His first experience on a shipwreck took place at Tobermory, Ontario, in the early 1980's, and he immediately fell in love with the history surrounding shipwrecks and the Great Lakes. He learned to take pictures underwater at the same time and combined diving and photography into a fantastic hobby. Perseverance and a lot of film resulted in an opportunity to display some of his photographs at the Underwater Canada Show in Toronto in 1984.

Since that time, he has spoken at numerous dive shows in Canada and the U.S.A. and shared his Great Lakes shipwreck experiences with other diving enthusiasts. Also, he has displayed his photos in books and magazines on numerous occasions. Most recently, his pictures of a tiger shark appeared in a dangerous marine creatures book published in the Netherlands. Diving has allowed him to explore many of the Great Lakes and has taken him to several far-off destinations including the Caribbean, the Bahamas, Bermuda, Hawaii and the South Pacific.

Stan Waterman's
Peerless Meatloaf

Stan Waterman in Toronto,
Canada, April 4, 1987.

"My wife, Susie, started the first organic food store in Princeton, New Jersey -- The Whole Earth Center. I haven't enjoyed eating at home since (only kidding). This recipe makes enough for two for dinner with enough left over to provide the meat for a spaghetti for two the following evening. I decided on broiling because so often meatloafs are dry and overcooked. I find a good Chilean Merlot goes wonderfully with it." -- Stan Waterman

Ingredients

1 1/2 lbs. ground sirloin

1 egg yolk

1/2 cup herb seasoned stuffing, ground fine

1/4 of a green pepper, chopped fine

1/4 of an onion, chopped fine

1 tablespoon mustard (Grey Poupon, of course)

Dash Worcestershire sauce

Salt and Pepper (heavy on the pepper)

Instructions

Combine all the ingredients in a mixing bowl. Mix it with your hands (don't be afraid -- go ahead and dig your hands in -- get messy). Form it into a loaf and put it in a baking pan with a spray of Pam under it.

Put it into the broiler and check it frequently. When black specks appear on the top of the loaf, take it out, turn it upside down and continue to broil until black specks appear on this side. It will still be medium pink on the inside and crusty and well done on the outside. If doubtful, open the loaf for inspection. If it is too rare, put it back into the broiler for another minute.

*This is a wonderfully innovative way to make meatloaf, especially if you like beef medium-rare. It's seared on the outside, tender and juicy on the inside, and altogether delicious.

Stan Waterman has been in the forefront of scuba diving since its inception as a recreational sport, in this country and throughout the world. His attraction to the underwater world began as a schoolboy in 1936 when he first dived with a Japanese Ama diver's mask in Florida. In the 1950's, inspired by Jacques Cousteau's revolutionary invention of the Aqua Lung, Stan acquired the first one in Maine and went on to pioneer scuba diving in that state.

Between 1954 and 1958, he operated a dive business in the Bahamas with a boat he had built specially for diving. His first 16mm film on diving was produced during those years. For the next 15 years, Stan continued to record his worldwide journeys and exploits on film; most were ultimately purchased as television documentaries. In 1965, he took his entire family - wife and three children - to Tahiti. Their careers as television stars were launched when National Geographic purchased the rights to air his film of that year-long experience.

In 1968, he collaborated with Peter Gimbel on the classic shark film, *Blue Water, White Death.* However, he may be best known for his work in commercial film. He was co-director of underwater photography in the production of *The Deep,* based on Peter Benchley's best-selling novel. In other collaborations with his close friend and neighbor, Mr. Benchley, he provided 10 years' worth of productions for ABC's "American Sportsman Show."

Stan has received honors and awards for his work in television and in behalf of the sea, including 5 Emmys, 2 Gold Medals from the U.K. Underwater Film Festival, 4 Golden Eagles, a Lifetime Achievement Award from the Miami Expo and from the Boston Sea Rovers, the Cousteau Diver of the Year Award, the Reaching Out Award from the Diving Equipment and Marketing Association, and most recently has been named to the International Scuba Diving Hall of Fame. The Discovery Channel produced a two-hour biographical special about Stan called *The Man Who Loves Sharks.*

Stan graduated from Dartmouth in 1946, where he studied with Robert Frost and earned a B.A. in English. He has maintained an appreciation of language and literature throughout his life. He is married and is the father of two sons and a daughter, each of whom has acquired a special love of the sea from him. He and his oldest son, Gordy, a successful cameraman in his own right, won the first father and son Emmy for their work together in the "National Geographic Explorer" production, *Dancing With Stingrays.* Stan maintains residences in New Jersey and Maine. Under the heading "Sea Salt," an article by Stan Waterman appears in each issue of *Ocean Realm* magazine. Stan continues to dive, film, lecture and host dive tours.

Photo submitted by Stan Waterman.

Emory Kristoff's
"Red Meat Diver's" Steak

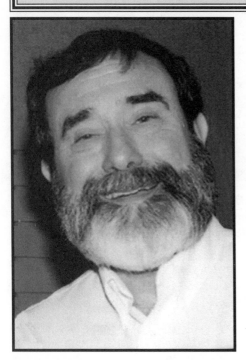

"I'm a red meat diver. However, in my line of work, going on expeditions to the far corners of the earth means that dining is a rather haphazard catch-as-catch-can affair. It tends to be meager and scroungy -- a matter of peanut butter and oatmeal, rather then haute cuisine. I travel on big ships where you're at the mercy of the expedition organizers. At least the Canadian Forces icebreakers have booze on board, unlike the Woods Hole ships. If I have control, I make sure there are steaks, lamb chops, ice cream and other good things. Basically, if it doesn't move faster than me, I can probably eat it." -- Emory Kristoff

Ingredients
1 excellent quality steak

Jerk sauce

Chocolate bar

Instructions
Smear jerk sauce all over the steak.

Grill to your own idea of perfect doneness.

Have the chocolate bar for dessert.

*Delicious in its simplicity! Expeditionary caterers, take note!

Emory Kristoff has been a National Geographic photographer ever since working for the magazine as an intern in 1963. Born in 1942, Emory graduated from the University of Maryland at College Park with a B.S. in journalism in 1964. A specialist in scientific, high-tech and underwater subjects, including Deep Ocean work beyond normal diver depths, he was a staff photographer from June, 1964 to October, 1994. He has worked as the special projects photographer since then.

Throughout his career, Emory has been a pioneer in the use of robot cameras and remotely operated vehicles. He created the preliminary designs of the electronic camera system for the Argo vehicle, which found the *Titanic*. He has led photographic surveys of the *C.S.S. Alabama* off the coast of France in 1992 and the 16th century wreck, *San Diego*, in the Philippines in 1993. In 1995, he led an expedition to recover the bell of the *Edmund Fitzgerald* and produced the first deep water images with High Definition TV.

His innovative photography uncovers the heretofore-unexplored worlds of the deep sea. "Testing the Waters of Rongelap," published in *National Geographic Magazine* in May, 1998, records oceanic life in the nuclear weapons contaminated waters surrounding the Marshall Islands. In August, 1998, Emory's pictures of the *Titanic* were presented in the *National Geographic Magazine* article "Tragedy in Three Dimensions." The pictures, recorded in 1991 using high-intensity lighting systems, appeared in unprecedented detail because of advances in 3-D computer video-editing.

Emory proudly wearing his Beneath The Sea medal, 1999.

Emory's accomplishments have earned him many awards for both writing and photography. In 1986, he and Robert Ballard [see his recipe on page 46] were awarded the American Society of Magazine Publishers Innovation in Photography Award for their photographic coverage of the *Titanic*.

Emory with fellow presenter Glen Egstrom [see his recipe on page 70] at Our World -- Underwater.

That same year, Emory earned the Explorer's Club Lowell Thomas Award for Underwater Exploration. In 1988, he was honored with the NOGI Award for Arts from the Underwater Society of America.

Emory Kristoff was presented the 1998 J. Winton Lemen Fellowship Award by the National Press Photographer's Association "for being one of our profession's most imaginative innovators with particular attention to pictures from beneath the ocean brought to the readers of *National Geographic Magazine*."

Hal Watts'
Steak To Dive For

"For many years I went to a restaurant in Orlando, Florida, that had the best steak I ever tasted. One of the waitresses had two kids that I taught how to scuba dive, and she gave me the recipe for the steak the way it was served there.

"I have travelled the world, I love steak, and I have found this to be the best." -- Hal Watts

Ingredients

T-bone steak

Adolph's un-seasoned tenderizer

Butter

Instructions

Baste both sides of the steak with tenderizer.

Punch in with fork.

Allow to set only 5 minutes. Not 5 minutes per side.

Smear with melted butter.

Pre-heat skillet with butter.

Sear both sides while skillet is hot.

Cook until desired doneness (I do mine rare).

Get ready for the smoke detector to go off - this can make some smoke! But it's worth it. Seared on the outside, pink and juicy on the inside - absolutely wonderful!

Hal Watts' first experience with scuba was in 1955 when he was working towards a Master of Laws degree in Atlanta, Georgia.

In 1967, he set a World Record Deep Air dive to 390 feet, which was acknowledged in the *Guinness Book of World Records.* As of early 2001, Hal held the World Record Deep Air dive in a cave to 415 feet.

He has trained six other world record deep air divers, including his daughter, Scarlett Watts, who, in 1999, established a new Women's World Record Deep air dive to 425 feet. She is in the Women Divers Hall of Fame.

Hal is an Extended Range Instructor Trainer for PSA, IANTD, NASE, NAUI, PDIC and TDI. He is also a Trimix Rebreather Instructor Trainer. In 1999, he was presented with the prestigious Beneath The Sea Diver of the Year Award for Education.

Hal's reputation of being one of the diving industry's foremost pioneers and authorities has

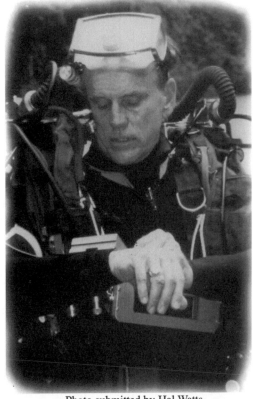

Photo submitted by Hal Watts.

afforded him the opportunity to dive all over the world. On July 4, 1990, Hal was one of the first recreational divers to dive on the Civil War ironclad, the *U.S.S. Monitor,* off Cape Hatteras, North Carolina. He had the privilege to be on the dive team with Gary Gentile [see Gary's recipe on page 18] and other deep wreck divers. Hal has also explored the *Andrea Doria* lying in 246 feet of water off the coast of New York.

Hal Watts has dived with sperm whales in the Azores, and explored the waters of Brazil, Italy, the Red Sea, Greece, Truk Lagoon, New Zealand, the Galapagos, Canada, the Aegean Sea in Turkey, and under the ice in Chicago. He has also worked as safety diver for record-holding free divers Tanya Streeter and Alejandro Ravelo.

In the 1960's, Hal introduced and named the "octopus" second stage, and he coined the phrase, " Plan Your Dive - Dive Your Plan." Hal is the founder of The Professional Scuba Association (PSA).

Jim Bowden's
Steak and Seduction

Jim Bowden talking business with the cookbook editor.

"This recipe is designed to be served as an intimate dinner, preferably for two, surprising even the most skeptical of women, that this guy does have some class. Accompanied by delicately done asparagus or snow peas and/or new potatoes modestly done and, presented with candlelight, it removes (at least temporarily) the belief that the dinner invitation was really just to get the lady into the cook's lair. A good Burgundy or Cabernet (French, "but of course," and a real cork, not a screw cap) is essential. The gentleman should choose music like Luis Miguel and resist the impulse to talk about how he narrowly escaped a dangerous entanglement while diving the *Titanic*. In fact, surprise her and inquire about her life, dreams and interests. It will surprise the hell out of her, and you might learn something about her that is as appealing as her physical charms. In fact, the likelihood of you getting to enjoy the latter is greatly enhanced by the former." -- Jim Bowden

Ingredients

3 tablespoons butter

2 filet mignons, cut 1 1/2 inch thick

1 teaspoon salt

1/4 teaspoon freshly ground black pepper

1/2 cup port

1/2 cup sautéed sliced mushrooms

3 tablespoons heavy cream

Instructions

Melt the butter in a skillet; brown the filet mignons in it over high heat 3 minutes on each side or to whatever desired rareness. Season with the salt and pepper and transfer to a heated serving dish; keep warm.

To the pan juices in the skillet, add the port, mushrooms and cream; cook over slow heat 3 minutes. Pour over the fillets.

A small garden salad to be eaten after the main course (like the French do. Vinegar dressings ruin the taste of the wine). Tell her that and she will be further impressed that her original opinion of you as a moron is perhaps incorrect.

Then serve her, you idiot. Don't yell for her to come load her plate.

Now, even if this does not get you romance every time, you can have the satisfaction of knowing that Emil Lagasse is a heart throb to a lot of ladies. It is going to work sometime.

*This is a delicious dish and easy to make. Be sure to follow all of Jim's instructions, especially the music, candles, and, most of all - listening to each other. It will be a lovely evening for both of you.

Jim Bowden is an explorer, full time. He is firmly committed to the underground. As founder and leader of the Proyecto de Buceo Espeleologico Mexico y America Central, he has lead small, highly committed expeditionary teams to Mexico, Belize and Guatemala to explore, survey and map water-filled caves. Much of his early work was solo. He was the outfitter for a Mexico expedition for the Museum of Natural History, Smithsonian Institution.

His current project site is the world's deepest known water-filled pit, Zacaton. In April, 1994, Jim successfully dove to 925 feet in this system and established a new world depth record on open circuit scuba. During 12 months of training prior to this dive, he became the first man to make multiple sub-500 ffw cave dives in one year. At present, he has made more sub-500 ffw dives on open circuit scuba than any man on record. Zacaton has been measured at 1,080 ffw.

Jim's future plans include the continued exploration of this world-class system and the extensive exploration of Mexico's deep river caves. Jim has published articles in multiple technical journals on cave diving and wilderness cave exploration. He is a cave diving

 instructor for NSS-CDS, NACD, NAUI, and TDI, but prefers to only be involved in teaching individuals who are dedicated and pursuing specific expeditionary goals in Science and Exploration. He is currently at work on a book chronicling his 20 years of travel and wilderness exploration in Central America.

Jim Bowden with colleague Bret Gilliam (right). See page 48 for Bret's recipe.

Bob Sanders'
South Pole-ish Pork

"In Antarctica, we don't have a barbecue, so we opt to broil our chops instead.

"Food prep in Antarctica is a bit different than in the states. As a researcher, time was limited, so quick, easy preparation was key. As you can imagine, frozen items were no problem, and with this environment--no bugs, no mold, etc. --our "freezer" was just a wood crate on the back step of our hut. If you can freeze it, we had it (except milk). On the other hand, fresh fruits and vegetables were scarce; they had to be flown in from New Zealand, and 'helicoptered' out to our remote field camp. Refrigeration, however, cold, not frozen, was more of a challenge.

Submitted by Bob Sanders.

"Defrosting took time, so we decided our dinners each morning, pulled in the meat to thaw, chipped ice for water, and *then* went to work. This pork recipe (a family secret...shhh) was easy, and ALWAYS a hit. Though barbecuing is best, the propane stoves were all we had down south, so broiling became an acceptable alternative. Though the memories will be different, I hope you enjoy this recipe as much as 6 hungry Antarctic researchers have!" -- Bob Sanders.

Ingredients

5 - 10 wafer-thin pork chops

1/2 cup honey

1/2 cup Kikkoman soy sauce

Instructions

Mix honey and soy sauce until single consistency. Pour over single layer of pork chops in pan or large ziplock bag. Marinate for at least 2 hours per side. Place on low heat BBQ and cook 5 minutes each side or until done.

Robert Sanders, D.M.T. (Diver Medical Technician), has over two decades of diving the waters of the planet, including 189 dives as a research diver and dive safety officer in Antarctica. Working for the New York State Dept. of Health, Sanders dove through 8-17 feet of polar ice in frigid 28-degree F. water, collecting single-cell critters!

He is currently pursuing a medical degree at Finch University of Health Sciences/The Chicago Medical School, and has worked as a motion picture medic and water safety coordinator. In his spare time, he volunteers as a Supervisor at the Catalina Hyperbaric Chamber and serves as a member of the Los Angeles Sheriff's Dept. Marine Company collecting evidence and victims from depth. His most recent project was perfecting dogtooth tuna sushi in Bikini Atoll.

Ann Kristovich's
Smokin' Ribs

"For me, cooking is a therapy most looked forward to after a busy time. I love nothing better than sharing the 'fruits' of my kitchen labors with friends. Good food in my book is right up there with good sex as things to hope for, and lessons to pursue. On that note, I am sending the most delicious pork rib recipe I have managed to produce. Just remember, they gotta be pork to be right." -- Ann Kristovich

Ingredients

1 3-1/2 lbs. rack of ribs, preferably not baby back (increase cooking time for heavier ribs)

RUB (Mix these rub ingredients in a small bowl):

1 tablespoon salt, sea salt or kosher salt

1 tablespoon good paprika, smoked if you can find it.

1 tablespoon brown sugar, packed

1 tablespoon fresh, coarse ground black pepper

1 teaspoon garlic powder

Instructions

Wash and dry the pork. Rub in the rub and set aside while you get the fire going. Make your fire so that the ribs will be as far away as possible from the direct heat. You can use all hardwood charcoal or a combination of hard wood charcoal and savory hardwoods to get your heat. Mesquite usually burns too long for this. Pecan, apple, hickory, oak all work well. You will need to maintain a smoker temperature of 250-300 degrees.

Put the ribs, bone down, on the racks as far from the heat as possible. Close the lid and smoke for 2 to 2 1/2 hours or until they get a good mahogany color. You may need to add fuel to the fire to maintain your heat. Wrap the ribs in heavy-duty foil and continue cooking for another hour. You will find that these ribs are fall-apart delicious. No sauce needed, but if you do, keep it on the side.

The smoky, delicious aroma coming from your grill will tantalize your guests!

Dr. Ann Kristovich is the co-leader of The Proyecto De Buceo Espeleologico Mexica Y America Central and has been involved in cave exploration since 1988 in Mexico, Belize and Central America. In 1993, she set a women's cave diving depth record of 554 feet (she became one of only six individuals in the world to have dove deeper than 500 feet at that time).

Ann is an instructor for IANTD, NSS-CDS, NACD, NAUI and TDI and teaches technical, deep, cave and mixed gas diving. Ann's articles and photos have been published internationally. Trained as an oral and maxillofacial surgeon, Ann serves as the deep-diving expedition team's doctor. She is an inaugural member of the Women Divers Hall of Fame.

FIFTH COURSE:
DESSERTS

"The idea of asking divers to share their favorite recipes seemed a little off at first, but then I thought about the average diver's waistline and the light went on. Dive equipment manufacturers tend to show off their latest creations close to, or draped across, the bodies of 20-year-old models with 4 or 5 percent body fat, tans and $12,000 worth of crowns glinting at the camera. We don't see many folks like that on dive boats here in the Great Lakes and the Atlantic Northeast. In fact, looking around at the usual suspects on the average weekend wreck-diving charter, I'm reminded more of a Hell's Angels convention than anything I ever saw in *Skin Diver* magazine. Tattoos and pants with elastic waistbands carry the vote, and there is no argument that a good part of the ton-and-a-half of gear and accessory boxes loaded onto the boat at dockside contain food, not dive gear." -- Steve Lewis [see page 10 for Steve's recipe.]

Don't worry about loosening the strap on your weightbelt -- just enjoy the desserts that our scuba diving celebrities have cooked up. After all, you've been a good diver all day -- you deserve it:

JOHN CHATTERTON's **Cut-The-Cheese Cheesecake** .... page 116

MICHEL GILBERT & DANIELLE ALARY's **Eggs in Maple Syrup** ...... page 118

GEORGIENNE BRADLEY's **Jungle Punch Jello** .... page 120

JAY IRELAND's **Mom's Tea Ring** .... page 121

NANCY & LARRY BOUCHA's **Purple Smile Blueberry Pie** .... page 122

KIMM STABELFELDT's **Chocolate Chip Cookies** .... page 124

John Chatterton's
Cut-The-Cheese Cheesecake

"I live on the beach, own three motorcycles, and dive deep wrecks. My wife, Carla, and I were married in a 1000-year-old Buddhist temple on a motorcycle trip through the mountains of Thailand and Burma. Traditional, we are not.

Her late mother, Eleanor, left her the official 'Oswald Family Cheesecake Recipe.' Great cheesecake, but way too stodgy for an Arlo Guthrie Thanksgiving at our house! Some minor changes in the ingredients, and a new name courtesy of my dive pal, Richie Kohler...and we have a real crowdpleaser, the <u>Cut-The-Cheese Cheesecake</u>. This is truly the best New York cheesecake. Virtually all calories." -- John Chatterton.

Left: With Atlantic Ocean shipwreck china after a recreational dive. Photo submitted by John Chatterton.

Ingredients

4   8-oz. tubs of whipped cream cheese

1/4 lb. of butter, softened

16 oz. sour cream -- room temperature

2 tablespoons corn starch

1 teaspoon vanilla

1 1/2 cups of granulated sugar

5 eggs -- room temperature

Instructions

Blend all ingredients except eggs.

After all the lumps are gone and all is completely blended, add the eggs -- one at a time -- and continue to mix well.

Pour mixture into a greased 10-inch springform pan.

Place pan into a large roasting pan that is half full of hot water.

Bake at 375 degrees for one hour.

Test with cake tester and remove when golden brown on top.

Cool cake on cake rack for at least one hour.

Serve plain or topped with your favorite fruit.

*Do yourself a favor. Go buy a springform pan and make this cheesecake. It's out of this world.

Captain John Chatterton has spent the last 20 years working as a commercial diver in and around New York City. Deep shipwrecks are where he takes his recreation. His discovery and subsequent identification of the German submarine, *U-869,* has been the subject of several

John Chatterton has a day job as a commercial diver. On September 11, 2001, he was working in the waters of New York Harbor; he was lucky to get himself and his crew out of the area with only the loss of one truck full of commercial diving equipment. Both photos submitted by John Chatterton.

television documentaries. He has participated in numerous international technical diving expeditions to the *RMS Lusitania, HMHS Britannic,* and the search for *Struma.* In 1995, he discovered and identified the World War I passenger freighter, *SS Carolina,* off the New Jersey coast, later recovering the Purser's safe and its contents of gold coins and diamond jewelry. He has made over 140 dives to the "Mount Everest of Wreck Diving," the *Andrea Doria.*

Michel Gilbert & Danielle Alary's
Eggs in Maple Syrup

"Maple syrup is a very popular fare in our province [Quebec]. I learned this recipe from my father who, a long time ago, used to cook in logging camps. This recipe is not fancy, nor is it light, but it provided a lot of calories for those who worked hard in the arctic-cold climate of Canadian winters. Moreover, once cooked, the preparation has quite a weird look and smells so-so, but...at least it is delicious, especially when served with some vanilla ice cream. It also has nothing to do with diving, but hey...I come from a landlocked region with a few hundred lakes and billions of maple trees." -- Michel Gilbert

Ingredients

1 can of maple syrup (3 cups minimum)

1 dozen eggs, beaten

Instructions

Pour the maple syrup in a cooking "pot."

Bring the maple syrup to the boiling point.

Cook the eggs "scrambled" style.

Once the eggs have the proper consistency, serve hot or cold.

For those who need the calorie intake, serve with a scoop or two of vanilla ice cream.

WARNING: The Surgeon-General has found that eating this stuff more than once a year may be hazardous to your health!

Use real Canadian maple syrup -- not the fake "maple-flavored" stuff. Children would love this! This is one of the few recipes that could be breakfast OR dessert!

Michel Gilbert and Danielle Alary are owners of SUB-IMAGES, a photography and multi-image production company and have been involved together in diving for more

than 20 years. Award winning speakers, writers and photographers, they have published more than 450 articles in various publications related to diving, travel and sailing. Sub-Images' editorial and photographic work is sold by 10 agents on all continents. They are underwater photography columnists for Diver Magazine in Canada. They have received, among other distinctions, the Canadian Diving Achievement Award (Canada East) in 1991 and the Diver of the Year Award for the Arts at Beneath The Sea in New York in 1995. In 1997, they won the coveted Silver Diver

Photo submitted by Michel Gilbert.

Award at the Antibes World Festival of Underwater Images. In 2000, Danielle chaired the photo jury at the Antibes World Festival of Underwater Images. In 2001, Danielle was inducted in the Women Divers Hall of Fame. Michel and Danielle were members of the jury in October, 2002, at the Antibes World Festival of Underwater Images.

Photo submitted by Danielle Alary.

Georgienne Bradley's
Jungle Punch Jello

Georgienne Bradley. Photo submitted by Georgienne Bradley & Jay Ireland.

"When I was on my first assignment for *Scuba Times* magazine, I had been sent to Costa Rica to bring back images. I was under a lot of pressure to succeed. By the time I finally got to the camp, I hadn't eaten anything all day. I'm one of those people who forgets to eat when I really get busy. At the camp I was offered 'Jungle Punch,' which tasted just great and I was thirsty. What I didn't know was that Jungle Punch is like a liquid jello laced with homemade jungle liquor. I'm not much of a drinker anyway. Was I sick! It was a rough night but the worst part was in the morning when I had to get on the whitewater raft!" -- Georgienne Bradley

Ingredients

1 small box of black cherry Jello

3/4 cup boiling water

3/4 cup Bacardi Light Rum

Instructions

Add the boiling water to the Jello to dissolve it. Once dissolved, add the rum. Mix and match, if you want. Then refrigerate. The squares remain rigid once set, and easy to cut and dispense.

Oh, is this good! Just be sure the kids don't think the squares of jello in the refrigerator are for them!

Georgienne Bradley began her photography career while working for the Cousteau Society as their Latin American representative. Scouring Central America for film concepts, she photographed a wide variety of animal life.

Jay Ireland has been a professional photographer for 8 years. As the owner of Ocean Images of Grand Cayman Island, Jay became a premier nature photographer above and below the waterline. In 1986, Jay noted the specialized behaviour of a population of stingrays and founded Stingray City in Grand Cayman. Today Stingray City is probably photographed more frequently than any other single underwater attraction.

Shooting underwater as well as on land, Jay and Georgienne have had work published in magazines such as *Time, Ocean Realm, Skin Diver, Scuba Times, Costa Rica Today,* and The Cousteau Society's *Calypso* and *Dolphin Logs.* Their wildlife photography has been featured on a series of national Postage Stamps and lottery tickets. They have published one book, *Cost Rica Photo Guide: Underwater* and are currently working on two more books.

Jay Ireland's
Mom's Tea Ring

"I began free diving in northern California when I was about 8 years old, bringing home ling cod and abalone. I came from a farm family where my mother commonly fed as many as 8 children since there were always cousins around. We lived in the country and my mother frequently made a 'Tea Ring' in the wood-burning stove for us. This recipe has been modified for modern stoves. Since I had so much responsibility as a child to hunt food for my family, I learned how to find and follow wildlife, so now I am able to capture wildlife on film." -- Jay Ireland

Jay Ireland. Photo submitted by Georgienne Bradley & Jay Ireland.

Ingredients

1 1/2 cup milk

1/2 cup sugar

2 teaspoons salt

1 stick margarine

1/2 cup warm water (108-115 degrees F.)

5 packages or cakes yeast, active dry or compressed

1 egg

4 cups unsifted flour

Instructions

Scald milk. Stir in sugar, salt and the margarine. Cool to lukewarm. Measure warm water into large, warm bowl. Sprinkle or crumble in the yeast. Stir until dissolved. Stir in lukewarm milk mixture, egg and half the flour. Beat until smooth. Stir in remaining flour to make a stiff batter. Cover tightly with waxed paper or aluminum foil. Refrigerate dough at least 2 hours.

Roll the dough out flat to about 1/8 inch. Put thin layer of butter about 2 cups. Sprinkle 3 cups of sugar, 2 cups of raisins, 2 cups of chopped nuts, and 2 tablespoons cinnamon. Roll into long roll and wrap inside a 14-inch cast iron skillet. Make 1-inch cuts halfway into the roll from the outside edge. To allow it to cook the inside, offset cut layers and bake at 350 degrees for an hour or until done. Let cool.

Topping: 2 pounds powdered sugar, 1 6-oz. can of evaporated milk, whipped together. Pour over ring while still warm to make glaze.

This is a delicious variation from the usual sticky buns. This recipe is so flexible that you can adjust the amount of sugar and butter after the rolling out to suit your own taste.

Nancy & Larry Boucha's
Purple Smile Blueberry Pie

"I have always scanned the newspapers for recipes -- of all kinds. Loving blueberries as I do, when I found this blueberry pie recipe from a family who has a Michigan blueberry farm, I grabbed it, and now I make it every year. I used to make six pies at a time, but that was a lot of pies for me and my roommate, and we ended up with blueberry pie for breakfast, lunch and dinner. One time, I brought a pie along when we went to Ravinia [outdoor theater for summer concerts near Chicago]. Do you know what happens to a pie when you're hiking around a park? It becomes blueberry crumble. But it tastes great anyway. When you're making this pie, eat any leftover sauce warm. You'll want to lick the pot." -- Nancy Boucha

Ingredients

1 9-inch deep dish pie shell, baked

4 cups fresh or frozen blueberries, divided

1 cup sugar

3 tablespoons cornstarch

1/4 teaspoon salt (less is fine)

1/4 cup water

Instructions

Line cooled pie shell with 2 cups blueberries.

To make sauce, cook remaining berries with other ingredients over medium heat while stirring until thickened (and purple).

Pour cooked sauce over berries in shell. Chill. Serves 6. A few blueberries more or less is fine. And if the berries are really sweet, you will want to use less sugar. Enjoy!

Note: If you are like most people in this day and age, you will be purchasing your pre-made pie shells at the grocery store. If so, they come in packages of two. So just double the above quantities. It is as easy as pie!

This is the absolute BEST blueberry pie I've ever tasted -- it's in a different class. I usually like to make my own pastry crust -- but this pie is all about the berries. The pie holds together well -- definitely <u>not</u> blueberry "soup" and the berries remain luscious and juicy.

Larry and Nancy Boucha have been shooting underwater images for over 20 years. Their work as owners of Scuba Systems Dive Center in Skokie, Illinois, lets them lead several dive trips a year. Whether on a shipwreck in Truk Lagoon or in Lake Superior, exploring a cave in Akumal or searching out bizarre marine life in Papua New Guinea, you can be assured that they will have camera in hand.

Larry, the technically oriented "Doctor Scuba," has long been involved in the design, modification, and repair of dive equipment, while Nancy has focused on the relationships and identification of marine life. As PADI Instructors, they enjoy sharing their knowledge with others. Larry is the Director of AV of Our World - Underwater. He won an Emmy for "A Fish Eye View" for Fox Thing in the Morning.

Their underwater photos and articles have been published by *Skin Diver* Magazine, in books, and by the Shedd Aquarium.

Larry & Nancy Boucha. Photos taken by Joe Oliver, Past President of the Underwater Archaeological Society of Chicago. Submitted by Larry & Nancy Boucha.

Kimm Stabelfeldt's
Chocolate Chip Cookies

"I've been making these cookies since my kids were small. Each Sunday, my three youngsters and I would make cookies, and these were the ones most often asked for. I kept making them even after my kids left for college, and I would ship them to the kids. After they completed college, they started doing serious diving with dad, and they always ask that I bring cookies on the dive trips." -- Kimm Stabelfeldt

Ingredients (makes about 6 dozen cookies)

2 3/4 cups all-purpose flour
1 teaspoon baking soda
1 teaspoon salt
1 cup or 2 sticks of butter or margarine -- use the good stuff
3/4 cup white sugar
3/4 cup brown sugar, packed

3/4 cup Quakers oats - do not use the cheap stuff
1 teaspoon cinnamon
1 teaspoon vanilla extract
2 large eggs
1 cup raisins
2 cups semi-sweet chocolate morsels
1 cup chopped nuts

Instructions

Preheat the oven to 375 degrees F. Combine eggs, both sugars and butter into a mixer. Mix. Then add flour, baking soda, vanilla extract, cinnamon and salt to the mix. Mix. Add the Quaker oats. Mix. Add nuts, raisins and chocolate chips. Drop rounded tablespoon of mix onto an ungreased baking sheet. Bake for 9 - 11 minutes. When done, remove from pan and repeat step above until all mix is gone or you have eaten all the dough.

Better double or triple the recipe when you make these for divers!

Submitted by Kimm Stabelfeldt.

Kimm Stabelfeldt holds one of the largest private collections of Great Lakes books and ephemera in Wisconsin and is the author of five popular Great Lakes dive guides. His work has been published in numerous periodicals and he holds memberships in many Great Lakes maritime organizations. A certified Divemaster and Trimix diver, Kimm is the President of Adventure Diving, Inc., a Great Lakes shipwreck dive charter service, and a Director of the Great Lakes Shipwreck Research Foundation, Inc., which runs the annual Ghost Ships Festival in Milwaukee. He holds degrees in Business and Computer Science and is an executive with a computer software company.

AFTER-DINNER MINTS

Clockwise from upper left: **Gary Gentile** looks the other way and hopes that others will, too, since he's eating food that did NOT float past his dive boat in the ocean. Maybe it was something he ate that made **Stan Waterman** give this reaction. **Wes Skiles** likes to eat seafood: "I see food and I eat it." So does **Ralph White**, who apparently viewed **Emory Kristoff's** BTS medal as food. Getting a recipe from some people was a challenge, and after a while, some scuba stars tried to hide whenever they saw Joan approaching. Who was that Mystery Man under that tablecloth at DEMA? **Bill Hamilton** couldn't find a tablecloth in time. **Pat Hammer** at "Our World--Underwater," like a deer caught in the headlights: BUSTED!

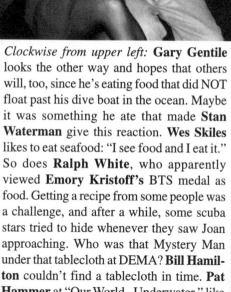

INDEX

A

Alary, Danielle, 118-119
Allen, Bob, 51
Allen, Rick, 64-65

B

Bachelor Delight, 54
Bachrach, Art, 24-25, 71
Bahama Island Lobster Boats, 50
Ballard, Robert, 46-47
Barbecued Narc-ed Fish, 74
Beer Butt Chicken, 88
Benchley, Peter, 105
Bimini Slaw, 34
Bird, Jonathan, 96-97
Boucha, Larry, 122-123
Boucha, Nancy, 122-123
Bowden, Jim, 20, 110-111
Boyd, Dick, 82-83
Boyd, Ellsworth, 50-51, 63
Bradley, Georgienne, 120
Breakdown Smorgasbord, 52
Brooks, Ernest, 56-57, 83
Brooks, John, 77
Burnham, Cindy, 64-65

C

Campfire Whitefish, 82
Cancelmo, Jesse, 92-93
Chatterton, John, 116-117
Chesnut, Gary, 44
Chicken in Cream Sauce, 86
Childs, Chet, 37
Chocolate Chip Cookies, 124
Chowdhury, Bernie, 22-23
Chunky Natsiq Soup, 26
Crowell, Dan, 60-61
Cut-The-Cheese Cheesecake, 116

D

DCS (Diver's Chili with Shrimp), 66
DeLoach, Anna, 12, 34-35
DeLoach, Ned, 12, 34-35
Diver's Delight Cucumbers, 38
Drafahl, Jack, 54
Drafahl, Sue, 54-55

E

Eggs in Maple Syrup, 118
Egstrom, Glen, 24, 25, 70-71

F

Farnquist, Tom, 18, 32-33
Feltner, Charles, 16-17
Feltner, Jeri, 16-17
"FishDan's" Delight, 72
Fisher, Mel, 73
Flavor Craver Shrimp Dip, 20
Flower Gardens Eggplant Parmigiana, 92
"For Treasure and Pleasure" Sea Bass, 80
Fried Smelt, Greek Style, 60

G

Gagnon, Dennis, 74-75

Gentile, Gary, 18-19, 83, 109, 125
Gilbert, Michel, 118-119
Gilliam, Bret, 48-49, 111
Gimbel, Peter, 105
Gray, Jeff, 88-89

H

Hackman, Gene, 77
Hamilton, Bill, 40-41, 125
Hammer, Patrick, 28-29
Hashed Shark, 62
Hayward, Joyce, 15, 30-31
"Hey Now!" Special Sauce, 68
Hot Lips Soup with Shrimp and Pork, 24
Huggins, Karl, 94-95
Humann, Paul, 12-13, 35

I

IFE New England Clam Bake, 46
Ireland, Jay, 120-121
Isle Royale Dip, 14

J

Jungle Punch Jello, 120

K

Keatts, Henry, 43, 58-59
Key West Clam Chowder, 28
Kohl, Cris, 9, 36-37, 99
Kristoff, Emory, 101, 106-107, 125
Kristovich, Ann, 114

L

LeBlanc, Ryan, 14-15
Lenihan, Dan, 76-77
Lewis, Steve, 10-11, 115
Long Island Scalloped Scallops, 58

M

Mango Manor Salsa, 12
Marx, Jenifer, 80-81
Marx, Robert, 80-81
McKenney, Jack & John, 20
Mixed Gas Chili & Beans (Titanic version), 100
Mom's Tea Ring, 121
Moore, Jeff, 84

N

Nawrocky, Pete, 52-53
New England Clam Chowder, 30

O

Old Baywatch Delight, 76
Oliver, Joe, 123
Olson Van Heest, Valerie, 90-91
Open Water Banana Split, 18
Orr, Betty, 66-67
Orr, Dan, 66-67
Outdoor Steamed Lobster, Maine Style, 48

P

Parry, Zale, 38-39
Peerless Meatloaf, 104
Perfect Perch/Awesome Abalone, 78

Purple Smile Blueberry Pie, 122

Q

R

Rapid Ascent Spaghetti Sauce, 94
Ravetch, Adam, 26-27
Razzle-Dazzle Sizzling Fish, 70
"Red Meat Diver's" Steak, 106
Road Kill Venison Stew, 84
Roduner, Vreni, 86-87

S

Salmon & Loosen-Your-Weightbelt Sauce, 55
Sanders, Bob, 112-113
Savory Salmon Sandwich, 44
Scallops a la "Just Love," 56
Shrimp and Grits, 64
Skerry, Brian, 42-43, 59
Skiles, Wes, 68-69, 125
Slaw, 36
Smokin' Ribs, 114
South Pole-ish Pork, 112
Stabelfeldt, Kimm, 124
Stayer, Jim, 98-99
Stayer, Pat, 98-99
Steak and Seduction, 110
Steak To Dive For, 108
Steele, John, 32
Steinborn, Bill, 20-21
Sterts, 90
Stoneman, John, 27
Stuffed Shells and Garlic

Bread, 96
Survival Grilled Cheese Sandwich, 42

T

Too-Many-Divers-in-the-House Chili, 98
Trotter, Dave, 84-85
Tucker, Teddy, 62-63
Tuna Surprise, 16

U

V

Van Heest, Jack, 91
Voodoo Onion Hummus, 10

W

Wachter, Georgann, 78-79
Wachter, Mike, 78-79
Wagner, Dan, 72-73
Wahl, Werner, 9
Waterman, Stan, 104-105, 125
Watts, Hal, 108-109
White, Ralph, 100-101, 125
Whitefish Point Whitefish Chowder, 32
Williams, Mike, 102-103
Winters, Chris, 33
World Class Tomato Sandwich, 40

X

Y

Z

Zesty Mariner's Meatloaf, 102

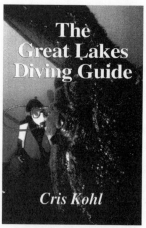

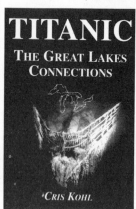
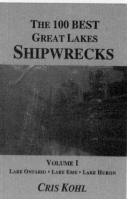
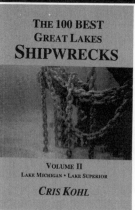
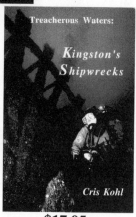